Human Dynamics in Construction Risk Management

– the key to success or failure

By
Charles O'Neil FCIArb
With Specialist Articles by 12 Industry Leaders

WWW.NXTBOOKMEDIA.COM

HUMAN DYNAMICS

IN CONSTRUCTION RISK MANAGEMENT | THE KEY TO SUCCESS OR FAILURE

Written by Charles O'Neil FCIArb
with Specialist Articles by 12 Industry Leaders

Author's Notes

All opinions expressed in the Contributors' chapters in this book are those of the authors and not of any organisation with which they may be associated.

All the other chapters that do not have a nominated author have been written by me, Charles O'Neil, and the opinions expressed in these chapters are mine alone and not of any organisation with which I am associated. The same applies to the quotations in boxes that have not been attributed to anyone in particular; some are commonly used in the industry and some are mine.

Notes on Project References

For obvious reasons we only refer to projects by name if the information quoted is publicly available on the internet from credible sources, such as from Company Announcements, Court Records, PPP portals, or approved in writing by the parties involved, and in each case we disclose the source.

Where the information is not publicly available, but we feel that important *"lessons learnt"* have occurred we describe *"anonymous"* projects. With these references the key facts that caused the situation are based on a real project in each case and are accurately described without any embellishment, but the names of the parties and the location are not mentioned.

Acknowledgements

Writing about the human aspects of risk management has been quite a challenge from the very start, even though it is a subject that has intrigued me for many years.

As ideas on how to put the human dynamics into context started to develop, I sought advice from a number of my colleagues. This advice was so helpful that the conversation then led to *"why don't you write a chapter?"*

So, we have ended up with 11 contributing authors and a Foreword by Peter Hansford and I would like to thank all of you very much, because there is no doubt that your experience and insights have given the book a much broader and more interesting perspective.

I would also like to thank all of my business colleagues and family members who have put in considerable effort in helping to get the book to the finish line.

With the editing and critiques, a special 'thank you' to Robert Gaitskell QC, Rob Horne, Hugh O'Connor and Ken Reid, to my wife Andrea for her support and meticulous attention to detail, and to all the contributing authors who provided many constructive comments. On the technical side my sons Derek and Charles Roger assisted greatly – thank you for your explanations and guidance.

With the production, thank you to Ben Edwards and Eve Au from Nxtbook Media UK and to Geoff Fisher and his team at CPI Group UK.

There have been many other helpful suggestions along the way from lots of people that I have not mentioned and I thank all of you very much.

Charles O'Neil
August 2014

List of Abbreviations

ADR – alternative dispute resolution
BBC – British Broadcasting Corporation
BMS – building management system
CBBC – Children's BBC
CPI – consumer price index
D&B – design and build
D&C – design and construct
DRB – Dispute Review Board
EOI – expression of interest
EOT – extension of time
FC – financial close
FF&E – furniture, fixtures and equipment
FFIP – fitness for intended purpose
FIDIC – Fédération Internationale des Ingénieurs-Conseils
(The International Federation of Consulting Engineers)
(The FIDIC suite of Contracts)
FM – Facilities Manager (also called Services Provider (SP))
GFC – global financial crisis
HS&E – health, safety and environment
ICC – International Chamber of Commerce
IRR – internal rate of return
IT – information technology (or independent tester)
JV – joint venture
LDs – liquidated damages
M&E – mechanical and electrical
NEC – The New Engineering Contract (The NEC suite of Contracts)
NPV – net present value
O&M – operations and maintenance
PC – practical completion
PFI – Private Finance Initiative
PPP – Public Private Partnership
QA – quality assurance
QS – Quantity Surveyor
RFP – request for pricing
RIBA – Royal Institute of British Architects
RM – risk management
ROI – return on investment
SP – Services Provider (also called Facilities Manager (FM))
SPC – special purpose company
SPV – special purpose vehicle
TA – technical adviser (or transaction adviser)
VO – variation order

Foreword

By Peter Hansford BSc MBA HonLLD FREng FICE FAPM
Chief Construction Adviser to the UK Government
President of the Institution of Civil Engineers 2010-2011

I have been deeply involved in risk management for construction projects and programmes since the early 1990s. This started when I was a reasonably young project manager on the Docklands Light Railway projects in London's East End, which included building new tunnels under some of the most expensive real estate in the world to construct a new station some 40 metres underground at Bank in the heart of the City of London. Tunnelling under the Mansion House and close to the Tower of London certainly opened my eyes to some of the wider risks associated with construction.

I was a founding contributor to RAMP – the Risk Analysis and Management for Projects handbook, first published in 1998 jointly by the Institution of Civil Engineers and the Faculty and Institute of Actuaries. This exercise was particularly interesting as engineers and actuaries address risk in very different ways.

In 2004 I was part of a team that reviewed the management of the Scottish Parliament Building project for the Auditor General for Scotland, leading on the project management and governance aspects. As with many projects that have overrun on their schedules and budgets, the reporting and management of risks was one of the key areas singled out for not being consistent with good practice.

And my involvement in reviewing project overruns continues today. At the time of writing this Foreword, I have recently been appointed to an Independent Expert Panel tasked with reviewing the Hong Kong section of the Guangzhou-Shenzhen-Hong Kong Express Rail Link. Examining the risk reporting and management systems and practices will certainly feature in that review.

Charles O'Neil has assembled an experienced and talented collection of contributors for this book, some of whom I have encountered and worked with at points during my career. Together they set out a valuable commentary to the key aspects of construction risk management and provide a strong endorsement of the central tenet of this book that effective management of construction risks is crucially dependent on people – their personal attributes, their interpersonal behaviours, their "human dynamics".

From my perspective as the Chief Construction Adviser to the UK Government, I firmly believe that the effective management of construction risks is not only important for the successful delivery of projects, but is also essential for the reputation of our global construction industry. The industry's reputation with investors, with governments and indeed with the general public is paramount for construction to play its part in the growth and maintenance of the infrastructure upon which society depends. We must be trusted to deliver, and that is a trust that we must earn.

I am pleased to commend this book to all students and practitioners of project and risk management.

Peter Hansford
August 2014

Biography – Peter Hansford

Peter Hansford was appointed Chief Construction Adviser to the UK Government in December 2012. He has over 35 years' experience in the development and delivery of major infrastructure projects, for governments, public and private clients, consultants and contractors in the UK and overseas. He has worked on highways, railways and energy projects in the UK, on new town infrastructure in Hong Kong and has advised on infrastructure developments and capital investment programmes for numerous clients. He is a Visiting Professor in the Bartlett School of Construction and Project Management at University College London.

Peter is a Fellow of the Royal Academy of Engineering, a Fellow of the Institution of Civil Engineers and a Fellow of the Association for Project Management. He served as the 146th President of the Institution of Civil Engineers from November 2010 to November 2011. He is Chairman of the charity, Engineers Without Borders UK. Peter was awarded the degree of Doctor of Laws honoris causa from the University of Nottingham in July 2014.

Introduction

Potential readers might well ask why the industry needs yet another book on construction risk management when virtually all organisations involved in the industry have systems and processes in place to protect their interests, be they developers, contractors, government authorities, investors and so on. Is there really a need for another book on this topic?

Construction, in all its forms from civil engineering to general building, is one of the world's biggest industries; a major employer, the generator of vast revenues and an economic barometer. Whilst the industry has made giant strides technically over the last few decades, in equipment, materials and techniques, it has surprisingly not made similar advances in effective risk management and projects continue to run off the rails worldwide every year and go disastrously wrong, both in developed and emerging nations.

In examining this problem from a practical standpoint, there are two obvious questions:

1. *"Why do project disasters continue to occur all over the world on a regular basis in this age of much more advanced management training?"*

2. *"High quality risk management systems are available, so what is going wrong with the application of these systems to prevent disasters and what can be done about it?"*

As an industry, we do not seem to have learnt from our mistakes over the years and continue to mess projects up badly. A significant factor might be the way in which we have been regularly changing the contractual arrangements between clients, contractors and other industry participants. Up until the 1980's it was easy to understand the system because the arrangements for most contracts were reasonably similar and achieved familiarity over years of use, however we now face different contractual circumstances almost every time. PPPs in particular are not a consistently moulded entity, with the arrangements, relationships, etc., differing widely and we also often deal with a new set of client personnel who have little project experience but are able to set their rules, leaving the contractors to handle the variances.

The ramifications of 'disaster' projects are widespread and include:

- Significant delays in the delivery of the proposed services
- Reduced returns on investment
- Claims and disputes, which are costly in both time and money
- Substantial losses for tenants and services contractors
- Breakdowns in business relationships
- Disruption to community services
- Political fallout and reputational damage
- High cost over-runs with heavy financial losses for investors, government clients, lenders, developers, contractors and insurers; and at worst,
- Bankruptcies for construction companies, subcontractors and suppliers

The following are recent examples of major project disasters and the publicly perceived reasons for their failures. The information quoted is readily available on the internet.

Berlin's New International Airport – currently three years behind program (2014) and reportedly more than €2bn over budget, including construction costs and compensation to services operators and retailers – the principle cause being the failure of the project management to comply with fire regulations plus a large number of functional design deficiencies that were unearthed late in the day; *http://en.wikipedia.org/wiki/Berlin_Brandenburg_Airport*

Edinburgh Trams, Scotland – more than three years behind program and reportedly costing three times the original budget of £375 million for a substantially reduced service – the principle causes are widely accepted as being poor political decision making and City Council inexperience in managing a project of this scale and complexity, with no significant blame being aimed at the contractors; *http://en.wikipedia.org/wiki/Edinburgh_Tram*

Australia – Wanthaggi Desalination Plant, Victoria, and Brisbane Airport Link – these two PPP projects have each incurred reported construction losses in excess of $500m, with the principle cause in each case being significant under-estimation of the primary costs and risks;
http://www.leighton.com.au/investor-and-media-centre/asx-announcements-and-media-releases
- Annual Report 29th Sept 2011 & subsequent reports

The above projects are large-scale examples in three different countries, but there are many more well-known examples around the world on projects of all sizes, including:

- Metronet and Tubelines, UK
  http://www.nao.org.uk/report/the-department-for-transport-the-failure-of-metronet/
  http://en.wikipedia.org/wiki/Tube_Lines
- Scottish Parliament Building, UK
- National Physics Laboratory, UK
  http://www.nao.org.uk/publications/0506/the_termination_of_the_pfi_con.aspx
- The Central Artery/Tunnel Project (the Big Dig), Boston, USA
  http://en.wikipedia.org/wiki/Big_Dig
- Hamburg Symphony Concert Building, Germany
- The Squaire Building, Frankfurt Airport, Germany
- Southern Cross Railway Station, Melbourne, Australia

Given these outcomes you would think that far more research, thought and practical effort would be dedicated to implementing more effective commercial risk management systems in order to reduce the probability of failure. To clarify, this book is principally about commercial risk management systems as distinct to health and safety risk, which is vitally important but rarely causes major project failure.

In all cases it is actually a failure of the project management application that is causing the problems. The risk management system should be able to expose the problems and rectify or mitigate them to an acceptable extent, but clearly this is not happening effectively.

Most of the examples referred to throughout the book come from large projects. That is because these are the projects with problems big enough to require careful exploration and they are projects that have attracted media attention, so the information used is publicly available. However, the principles involved remain the same for all size projects, albeit on a different scale.

http://www.globaltimes.cn/NEWS/tabid/99/ID/762900/Brisbanes-Airport-Link-biggest-construction-project-disaster-ASA.aspx February 20, 2013

The Australian Shareholders Association (ASA) has described **Brisbane's Airport Link as the "biggest construction project disaster" in recent history**, local media reported on Wednesday.

Queensland toll road operator BrisConnections was placed in administration on Tuesday

seven months after opening, with debts totaling more than 3 billion AU dollars (3.1 billion US dollars) according to the Australian Broadcasting Corporation (ABC). The receivership came after traffic flows only reached less than half of what was projected.

ASA spokesman Stephen Mayne told ABC radio that the failure of BrisConnection was more significant than others.

"For the builders to lose a billion, the investors to lose 1.2 billion AU dollars, and the bankers to lose between 1 billion AU dollars and 2 billion AU dollars, that's just a fiasco," he told ABC radio. "Clearly the Macquarie Bank and Deutsche Bank which put it together initially were far too optimistic and were driven by a pre-GFC (global financial crisis) mentality."

The Importance of Human Dynamics in Risk Management

A common factor in risk management is human dynamics and this book explores how and why **people are the problem in many instances, not a lack of effective risk management systems,** of which there are plenty, with most companies either using a proprietary system or having developed their own in-house versions.

It is recognised that many people in the industry all over the world have been concerned for a long time about how to more effectively manage the human dynamics of risk management, so it is amazing that so little has been done on an industry basis to tackle the 'people problem' from a practical viewpoint.

In the widespread research for this book, my co-authors and I have come across surprisingly little written on the human behavioural aspects of risk management, but we do wish to give credit where it is due and refer readers to the links to three relevant Papers in Appendix C. No doubt there have been other Papers written on the subject that we have not come across and to the authors of any such Papers our omission to mention you is only because we have not come across your work.

So why do **human dynamics** interfere so often with risk management systems to the detriment of a project? The following pages show how this happens at all levels, from the assistant surveyor or site manager, to estimators, commercial and legal managers and advisors, with senior management and all the way through to the Boardroom. The book then goes on to provide analyses, answers and recommendations to try and overcome the problem.

The Structure of the Book

The *'story board'* covers the following topics:

- ▶ The central theme – how human dynamics affect the success or failure of projects
- ▶ Key ingredients and examples of successful projects
- ▶ Common causes of project failure
- ▶ Changes to the industry and the way it operates today
- ▶ Structuring projects, including contracts and the administration
- ▶ Effective operational risk management
- ▶ Methods for resolving issues and avoiding formal disputes
- ▶ The value of independent oversight
- ▶ Practical human resources considerations

Practical recommendations are included in all sections of the book.

The Scottish Parliament Building

I have lost quite a bit of sleep pondering over how to convey my thoughts in this book. It is all very well to believe from experience that people are the problem and not the processes, but how to write a convincing and logical story on this is quite difficult. As an arbitrator I know the importance of providing full reasoning based on a clear and objective assessment of the facts and evidence, all black and white and with no room for personal bias or emotional interpretation.

It has proven to be difficult to clearly establish evidence and build the reasoning to support our contentions in regard to the effects of human dynamics in the industry. Is the lack of research and written material on this subject because others have also found it a difficult topic to express in words?

This book is primarily about how people react in certain situations under pressure or for other extraneous reasons. We look at all levels of personnel from Board members to site managers. We delve into a range of human behaviour, including defensiveness, aggression (bullies and sledge-hammer managers), greed, ego driven behaviour, loss of perspective and reality and bottom-drawer managers who hide or ignore things for different reasons.

We have chosen to use the term *'human dynamics'* because it depicts the much wider implications that flow on from the different types of human behaviour and human factors that individually affect each situation.

In order to properly analyse and understand how human dynamics affect risk management, it is equally important to examine successful projects as well as those that get into serious trouble, so that effective comparisons can be made and the differences properly understood. Chapters 4 to 10 look at these differences.

With all projects, whether successful or otherwise, whether publicly or privately controlled, it remains a fact that the outcome is a direct reflection of the human inputs at the different levels of management. *It is also a fact of life that that whenever there is a problem it can invariably be traced back to a breakdown in communication or reporting somewhere that overrides the risk management controls.* This is a human problem and the best systems and processes in the world will not overcome it. The challenges of communication are demonstrated even in this book, with standardisation of terms, e.g. with some authors using 'schedule' and some using *'program'*.

When a strong-minded project manager overrides or ignores fundamental issues such as compliance with fire regulations, it still amounts to a breakdown in communications because either the reporting systems or other stakeholders have not sounded the alert to responsible personnel further up the chain of command. As another example, mid-level managers can sometimes be a problem if they have a misguided ego-driven sense of power and enough autonomy to block communications up and down the company's communication and reporting chain.

The Need for a New Approach that Recognises and Limits the Potential Impact of Erroneous Human Behaviour in Construction Processes

Given the scale of the problem, there is a clear need for more in-depth practical guidance on how to identify the ways in which human behaviour can often interfere with risk management to the detriment of a project. It is not hard to demonstrate that this takes place at all levels, but it is certainly difficult to eliminate or even substantially reduce the effects of such erroneous human behaviour.

With the continuing run of project disasters around the world every year, it is quite apparent that there is a need for a new approach to risk management that places much greater importance on the role of human behaviour in the bidding, design and construction processes for major projects.

An effective risk management structure should expose these detrimental human behaviour situations quickly and before real damage is done.

What areas of risk management are we talking about?

Risk management covers any potential issue that is likely to jeopardise the project at any stage of its life, including but not limited to the following list.

Essentially, those issues that are the most vulnerable to 'human' related faults are:

- Overly optimistic bidding through under-pricing or a failure to understand the full requirements of the Bid (e.g. to include statutory approvals or accept geophysical risk) - i.e. establishing an unrealistic Bid pricing build-up, which results in a dangerously false picture. The causes can range from commercial or political pressures (maybe not even consciously) to a failure to manage the Bid properly, or just incompetence.

- Unrealistic and unrepresentative project reporting, possibly continuing the unrealistic structure and pricing of the Bid and failing to speak up, or an unwillingness to recognise and reveal problems, or **the misguided intent of keeping quiet and fixing problems at project level alone** (this is a particular problem that occurs regularly and risk management reporting needs to be designed to eliminate it). *Many project managers fail to recognise that by reporting a potential risk they obtain the assistance of the wider management team and no longer carry the worry alone,* with the possibility of jeopardising their job. Mostly it is an ego driven problem.

- Failure to create the team and integrate it together. One of the worst problems that we give ourselves is to set out on a new enterprise (huge in its size and complexity) with completely new groups of people and organisations, with no established pattern or idea for how the management systems will be put together and run – it's a recipe for disaster.

- Failure to manage the work properly; this leads to failure to adhere to normal standards and practice even when they are in place, (i.e. HS&E, QA, use of codes of practice, etc.). The lack of supervision and management sends the wrong message to staff and fails to identify problems and catch them before they become a disaster.

- Failure to produce realistic budgets and control of costs and margins, maybe to conceal the likely truth in order to get approval or maybe through inefficiency or incompetence.

- Poor cash flow management and unrepresentative financial reporting.

- Planning and programming, including failure to work through the detailed program exercise from an early stage (i.e. plugging in durations that turn out to be far more complex and critical than envisaged).

- Resource allocation generally – key people suitability, all personnel, consultants, plant and equipment, i.e. a lack of competent people, staff shortage and staff who do not recognise or take responsibility.

- Failure to have good people management and personal motivation, team spirit development and employee satisfaction.

- Project meetings – a lack of scheduled mandatory meetings with specific purposes, involving all stakeholders and with accurate Minutes distributed promptly. The key emphasis here is the challenge of getting all the right people in the right place at the right time. This is often difficult when dealing with multiple parties and failure to have a fixed meeting schedule results in absences of key people and communication gaps.

- Quality assurance – failure to diligently and methodically conduct continuous QA inspections and reviews; and a failure to understand the significance of *'doing it right the first time'*.

- Effective communications are essential for success, otherwise stakeholder and business relationships will suffer, together with reputations.

- Authority approvals – a failure to adequately identify all that are required and have them timeously approved causes huge delay, leading to loss of income, liquidated damages, loss of confidence and credibility, decaying staff morale, etc.

- Health, safety and environment – all have greatly increased importance globally and failing to recognise this can be very expensive, both in physical and monetary terms.

- Issues and claims – failure to proactively manage them can turn them into disputes, quite unnecessarily and at considerable time and cost.

- Corporate governance breakdowns, e.g. breaches of bank covenants.

- Corporate social responsibility; community and political considerations – ignore these at your peril.

- Task management – one of the keys to eliminating risk is to have an automated system for generating/reminding people of tasks that are due or close to due, e.g. Affinitext Task Manager – ensuring Contract obligations are met on time and not overlooked.

With all the above risk management areas, clients and contractors mostly put the processes in place, but it is the failure of people to take responsibility and to do what they know is needed that allows disasters to develop.

The prime objective of this book is to identify and analyse the human involvement in all these areas and show how these personal behaviours affect the success or failure of construction projects. Then, from this make recommendations on how corporate processes can be developed to counter and control the issues that arise from these different behaviours.

In summary, the contents of the book cover the following three main areas:

- A general explanation of how erroneous human behaviour can interfere with risk management processes to the serious detriment of a project (Chapter 10);

- Conversely, how successful projects are the direct result of excellence in the different aspects of personal inputs and behaviours, particularly in the areas of communications and relationship management at all levels (Chapters 4-8);

- A range of solutions and best practice guidelines to safeguard projects through robust risk management that combines technical processes with excellence of the human inputs at all levels (Chapters 14-21 and 27-28).

History has proven that this is not an easy task however the author and contributors to this book hope that the contents will provide a meaningful and practical contribution to helping the construction industry become more efficient and less risky for clients and contractors through a more in-depth understanding of the human dynamics that are involved.

One of our key objectives in this book is to make the *'lessons learnt'* available in an easy-to-read, concise and practical form, so that young managers in the industry can take them on board and avoid making the same mistakes as their predecessors.

The Target Audience

Being such a large global industry, there is the wide range of stakeholders and parties with an interest in major projects, in particular senior management and decision makers at all levels that have an input into the procurement and delivery of projects, from Board members to site managers.

A key objective of this book is to provide information that will be of benefit to industry participants in both developed and developing countries, including the following people:

- University students – engineering, architecture, law, finance and commerce
- Post-graduate students
- Graduate engineers and trainee project managers
- Business development managers
- Legal and financial advisors; bankers
- Estimators, programmers and quantity surveyors
- Finance and accounting managers
- Risk managers and controllers
- Procurement and construction managers
- Facilities management and industrial services managers
- Regional and general managers
- CEOs and Board members
- Public servants
- Clients
- Politicians
- Dispute resolution professionals
- Internal and external auditors
- Industry and financial journalists

My Journey towards understanding Risk Management – from the Australian Bush to International Construction, Asset Management & Dispute Resolution

By Charles O'Neil DipArb FCIArb
Director Contract Dynamics Consulting

Every journey has a departure point and possibly a number of destinations en-route. Mine started 400 kilometres west of Sydney in Australia and I have lived and worked in several countries and localities en-route. In 2014, the year in which this book is being published, I am currently living in Germany, but lucky enough to be travelling to various places around the world on a regular basis.

I grew up on my parents' 4,000 acre farm west of Sydney and rode a horse to a one-teacher bush primary school five kilometres down the road, with 16 pupils. After primary school I went to Sydney to board at The Scots College for my secondary schooling, successfully passed the final year exams and left school at 16. My exam results were good enough to go to university, but this was never considered and I went back to the bush to learn about sheep, cattle and farming, often spending long days on horseback. Somehow it seems ironic that more than 30 years later and after many winding roads I decided it was time to go to university and enrolled at Reading University in the UK to study Arbitration Law and Practice.

The year after leaving school I toured the world for 6 months playing 1st grade cricket with an Australian Club team in 12 countries from Canada to Sri Lanka, with the UK being the main destination. This was undoubtedly an influential point in my life as it opened my eyes to the fact that there was a lot more to the world and set the stage for my later international career.

I then worked with my father on his farm for four years, during which time I learnt to fly and then went 500 kilometres further north to manage a 7,000 acre sheep and cattle property. My pilot's licence became important some years later when I entered the construction industry and was managing projects in remote areas.

I liked tinkering with and repairing machinery, welding and building steel yards and sheds on the farms and in 1969, I was co-inventor with another farmer of a new type of steel cattle crush, used for administering veterinary treatment to cattle in large numbers. We both needed one, but couldn't afford the existing models and in any case thought we could design a better one. On the back of this we commenced a manufacturing business and within 6 months had 25 employees. I bought out my partner and expanded the range of equipment and also moved into commercial steel fabrication. In 1972 and in 1974, I won awards for new equipment design at the Australian National Field Days, an annual show for farmers and stock breeders.

In 1974, I obtained my Construction Supervisor's certificate and Builder's Licence and our business entered into general construction. We expanded to 100 employees and completed our first significant project that year, the structural framework for a 30,000m² shopping centre, which we built in record time. We entered into a penalty/bonus contract, with my team taking 90% of an attractive performance bonus and the business keeping 10%.

This seemed to set the scene for the direction of our business, which from then on concentrated on what we termed 'performance contracting'; undertaking D&C contracts in Australia and New Zealand with demanding programs and fixed lump sum contract prices. At the same time we undertook some property development with retail, commercial and residential projects. Through this we gained experience in concept design, feasibility studies, financing and facilities management. As our "own" builder we quickly learnt the importance of the S-Curve when projects are being developed on loan finance (see chapter 21).

In 1990-91 Australia was in the grip of a recession, the construction industry was at low ebb and it was hard to obtain new projects, let alone make a profit. However south-east Asia was booming so I toured several countries looking for opportunities and in early 1992 signed an Agreement with a Vietnamese government company in Ho Chi Minh City to finance, design, construct and operate a 21 level serviced apartment development. It was a 30 year contract that was effectively a Public Private Partnership. This was one of the first joint ventures established after Vietnam opened its doors to direct foreign investment and it was not an easy road. The joint venture agreement, planning and building approvals and financing took two years to finalise, but the project was successfully completed in September 1996 and continues today as one of the most successful joint ventures in Vietnam.

This was the start of my international career in managing developments and construction projects. Prior to this I had undertaken consulting and lecturing during the `Eighties in China, India, Sri Lanka and Indonesia, but had not been involved in direct management of projects. The high-rise construction project in Vietnam presented a huge learning curve for me in respect of understanding and managing a project involving multi-national participants, contracts and financing.

I lived in Ho Chi Minh City for five years and then in Kuala Lumpur for four years. My involvement in design and construction during this time included factories in Vietnam for foreign manufacturers, shopping centre and industrial park developments in Malaysia and the infrastructure and utilities design for a new 500 acre township near Yangon in Myanmar, completed before the international sanctions were put in place. These activities introduced me to a broad range of interesting companies, design consultants and government organisations in these countries and in Singapore and Hong Kong.

Looking back, the most significant experience that I gained was an understanding of the diverse cultural and business practices in the different Asian countries I worked in – and they really are different. It is no more appropriate to refer to "Asia" as a culture than it is to talk about a "European" culture; in each region there are as many cultures as there are countries.

In 2001, I joined the German company Bilfinger SE in the UK, in their PPP division. To me this was a great challenge because PPPs incorporate all aspects of the development and construction industry, including design, feasibilities, financing, comprehensive contract documents, 'performance' construction and the ongoing operations of the facilities. PPPs are partnering in the true sense and if you don't get it right then the financial and reputational losses can be heavy. The ingredients for successful PPPs are well covered in this book in several chapters, but in short PPPs are all about people and the projects rely heavily on the human dynamics working in a positive manner.

Over the next 11 years I worked on a wide range of PPPs in the UK, Europe, Australia, Canada and Chile and enjoyed every moment of it. There were times when I needed to call on my performance contracting experience to expedite projects to meet target opening dates, because running late is not an option with PPPs – and not just for *'return on investment'* reasons.

There can be some very real human reasons. For example, take a new maternity hospital that is replacing three worn-out old hospitals. The Health Authorities publicly announce the Opening Date six months ahead and at the same time send out letters to 1,000 pregnant mums advising them they can have their babies in the new hospital. Three months down the track the builder says he will be a month late. NOT ACCEPTABLE. I was not going to face those pregnant mums! The hospital opened on time!

Acceleration is a fine line between achieving the target date and blowing the budget, but it does not have to be all about throwing money at it to fix it; in fact there is a much better way. If you lead from the front, motivate and encourage your management team, the builder and their subcontractors, it is not too hard to develop a broad team spirit whereby no one wants to be the one that lets the team down. People really will go that extra mile on this basis. Empathy, relationships and communications are all-important.

During my time working with Bilfinger on PPPs, I became more and more interested in risk management and how vital it is to understand the human element. In 2009-11, I was director of asset management for the Bilfinger global infrastructure portfolio, overviewing design and construction and operational performance of a range of investments in several countries, including motorways and bridges, hospitals, schools, prisons, and government administration buildings. During this period, I led a team that restructured the global financial and operational reporting into a standardised real-time process and implemented stringent *"look-ahead"* risk management procedures.

My interest in dispute resolution goes back a long way because of my involvement in contracting. In 2001, I commenced studying arbitration law and practice at Reading University in the UK. This was a challenging four years whilst working at the same time, but it was very worthwhile. The principles of arbitration that you learn change the way you approach a problem, be it in construction or any form of business.

You learn to be more *'black and white'* objective in unearthing and assessing the facts and not to be confused by emotional and self-interested interpretations; to view things impartially; how to read contracts and determine the rights and obligations of the parties, and so on. It can be recommended as great training at any stage in your career, even if you never go on to be an active arbitrator.

So how does this fit in with the *'human dynamics'* perspective? I think it makes you more aware of the effects that human behaviours have on situations and how vital it is to understand this in establishing robust risk management.

My observations and commentary now about risk management are wisdom in hindsight based on years of observing people in action and some hard personal learning experiences *('bought experience')*. In my earlier days I did not really comprehend the significance of anticipatory risk management and as a contractor, I got a real challenge and buzz out of being a *'performance contractor'*, taking on contracts with very tight programs, but always concentrating on high quality and *'doing it right the first time'*. Along with a dedicated and highly motivated team, this was our method of risk management, even if we didn't recognise it at the time.

However, looking back, this combination of *'bought experience'* and observing the behaviour of others proved to be invaluable as my career progressed. It is worth mentioning that a lot of my experience involved industrial relations conflict with the unions. The Australian construction industry was almost in a state of warfare with the construction unions in the 1970's and 80's, with constant strikes and disruptions emanating from logs of claims from the unions for better pay and conditions. Some of it was justified, but much of it wasn't and was the result of having three different construction unions battling each other in a turf war for control of segments of the industry or specific sites.

I have been very fortunate in having had the opportunity to have had a wide range of varied experience and I have come to firmly believe that a proper level of communication is the key to strong project performance, reducing the risks and resolving issues before they turn into formal disputes. I will always *'talk, talk and talk some more'* in an effort to settle claims and disputes in order to stop them going to the expensive exercise of litigation, arbitration or other forms of alternative dispute resolution. This may seem contradictory to my being an arbitrator, but it is probably a reflection of the hard lessons I learnt as a contractor.

I decided to write this book after concluding at some stage that *"people are definitely the problem, not processes"* and that the big question is how to reduce the potential for individuals to sidestep the system and cause all sorts of problems through their erroneous behaviour.

I wish to wholeheartedly thank my co-authors for joining with me to make a meaningful contribution towards more effective and positive human dynamics in the construction industry.

We have seen many changes take place in the industry during the course of our careers, especially since the 1980's, and it is important to understand why and how these took place as many of them have related to the human behavioural issues raised in this book. Unfortunately, it appears there is still a long way to go. Chapters 11-13 summarise the most significant changes that have taken place in the construction industry in recent times.

Key Ingredients of Successful Projects

Centennial Bridge Panama Canal - an outstanding success, based on good planning, built in 29 months, opened in 2004

So what happens on the good projects? What are the key areas and actions that create success?

Before looking at this, we need to first define *"success"*. It is generally agreed in the industry that we should aim to achieve the following:

- Build a quality project that meets the aesthetic, technical and functional requirements of the client
- Deliver on time and on budget
- An acceptable level of profit and return on investment (ROI) for all stakeholders
- Good communications, cooperative meetings and respectful relationships
- Issues and claims resolved by sensible negotiation; no formal disputes
- Job satisfaction, adequate rewarding remuneration for all employees
- Strong team spirit amongst the stakeholders
- Smooth operations from a technical point of view after completion of construction
- End-users that are very pleased with their new facilities in all respects

Successful projects are the result of careful planning, realistic contract prices and programs, robust specifications and contract documents and having in place the right management teams and processes. In other words, all the right components are in place.

The following elements for success are fundamental, but it should be remembered that they all have potential for risk and this must be kept in mind and reviewed on a constant basis.

- Careful planning and programming (see Chapter 21 re the significance of the S-Curve)
- Sensible and achievable cost plan; contract pricing with a realistic build-up and acceptable margins (do not 'buy' work, because Murphy's Law is bound to apply)
- Properly detailed specifications and contract documents (spend extra time on this – it's worth it)
- Design development running in close parallel with cost planning
- Good leadership and competent, professional teams for all stakeholders
- Efficient contract management platforms, with well-documented systems and processes – a common failure arises with staff turnover – it is important to document the way things are done so that knowledge is retained and easily transferable when staff leave
- Good communications protocol, respectful relationships and sound relationship management
- A proactive level of participation and cooperation by all stakeholders
- Clear project objectives that are realistic and achievable, including design, budgets and programs, backed by strong team spirit from all stakeholders
- Healthy project cash flow, with head contractor payments in line with program;
- Satisfactory supplier and subcontractor payments
- Head contractor, suppliers and subcontractors all satisfied with their margins
- All parties having a detailed knowledge of their contract documents and contractual obligations (PPPs in particular)
- Professional consultants and efficient subcontractors that deliver quality work on time

You will note that all of the above areas have a strong human element and it is almost taken for granted that the teams involved will be right on top of the technical aspects.

If any of these areas are badly structured or handled, then the effect on the overall project can be serious.

It is vital that there is robust risk management throughout the life of the project, with the key methodology being early warning through constant monitoring and anticipation, together with an inclusive stakeholder communication process.

A perfect project is when people say
'Weren't they lucky to have such a smooth run – what did they do to earn their money'
But it has nothing to do with luck!

Examples of Successful Projects and How They Managed Risk

There is no better way to learn how to run a successful project than to participate in one personally. If this is not possible initially then hearing how to do it from highly successful senior managers is the next best way.

In this section of the book we are privileged to include the following three Papers from industry leaders describing how they achieved success with their high profile projects.

► MediacityUK (BBC North)
► Royal Women's Hospital, Melbourne, Australia
► London 2012 Olympic & Paralympic Games

MediacityUK (BBC North) as a Model Project

By Stephen Warburton BA(Hons), DipArch, MSc, RIBA
Former Senior Design Manager, Lend Lease Corporation, UK

"Who would have thought the BBC would be the catalyst for a complete city [Mediacity] in less than seven years. It goes back to my core idea that if you get a few good people working together and willing to partner effectively, you can create great things."

Chris Kane, Head of BBC Property, Building article 8 February 2013

The decision to create MediacityUK, on a 15 ha area of derelict wasteland in Salford, 2 miles from the centre of Manchester, was in direct response to Tony Blair's post 9-11 security proposals to safeguard the UK's key broadcaster, the BBC, by making it less *'London-centric'*.

A budget of £233m was allocated for the BBC to move several departments (including BBC Sport and Children's BBC) to Salford. The outturn cost was £9m lower than this, and Lend Lease delivered the project ahead of schedule. It should be noted that the overall build and infrastructure cost was £650m, including a new Metrolink Tram stop and an outdoor 'piazza' larger than Trafalgar Square. The BBC's total budget for moving to Salford and operating the site to 2030, (when the BBC lease on the site ends), is £942 million.

The developer, Peel Group, had won the rights to develop the site after beating off a rival bid from central Manchester in 2006. My involvement, from the summer of 2006, was to lead the pre-construction design management process on behalf of Lend Lease, made trickier by the fact the original winning scheme was 'ripped up' and a new limited competition issued to design the three BBC buildings. Wilkinson Eyre were the winning architects, their excellent project architect, Giles Martin, had also designed Berlin's Reichstag for Sir Norman Foster, opened in 1999.

MediacityUK (BBC North), Dec 2008

The establishment of a close-knit team comprising Developer/Tenant (BBC)/Contractor from an early stage was key in managing the risks associated, both with radical re-design and the pace of design needed to hit a targeted Lease Agreement date of May 2007.

The BBC themselves should take credit for fostering a collaborative approach to the design and construction process. We alternated meetings between Peel's offices at the Trafford Centre in Manchester, and the BBC offices at Television Centre and White City in London. The London trips were by far the most inspiring. Each was augmented by a fairly well planned indoctrination into the BBC's world of broadcasting, from seeing live filming of Blue Peter by CBBC, seminars by the BBC's security and acoustics experts, and trips to BBC Scotland nearing completion and also delivered by Lend Lease. The BBC project team were clearly enthusiastic and proud of the moniker of 'world's best broadcaster'. There was an infectious spirit to visiting great quality buildings with them, Chipperfields BBC North in Glasgow, Allies and Morrison's White City Development, McCormac Jamieson & Pritchard's Broadcasting House. One got a feeling the BBC was setting the bar in terms of architectural quality and I felt it was my role to spread this message amongst my management colleagues at Lend Lease, in order that expectations followed through to the supply chain.

So, why was this period of familiarisation so important? Well, firstly it bonded the team towards a common goal and gave us ownership. Secondly, it raised everyone's technical knowledge considerably and allowed us to discuss the project with authority outside of the group. It was the human dynamic element that reduced the opportunities for misunderstanding or misrepresentation of design intent and construction delivery goals. Could the project have been delivered as successfully if say Peel had taken a more traditional approach of keeping the tenant at arms-length and project managed directly. I don't think so. In order to make the development a functional success overall (bearing in mind the scrutiny that the BBC is constantly under vis spending license payers' money) far too much of detailed understanding of the tenants' operational broadcast activities was needed to enable the project to be undertaken using the more traditional approach.

Some issues of design flexibility had raised their head at BBC Scotland, although the design was only a couple of years old, technology had advanced by such a degree in 2006 that what was previously only possible in a soundproofed editing suite, with many thousands of pounds worth of equipment, could now be done on laptops. BBC Scotland was clearly a smaller (£72m) testbed for many of the ideas employed in making the larger project in Salford a success. The knowledge I gained from my counterpart, Roy Allport in Scotland was invaluable. (Roy now heads the Lend Lease business in Scotland).

By the time Christmas 2006 arrived the project was in good shape, a robust RIBA Stage D design had been delivered by Giles at Wilkinson Eyre that met the BBC's aspirations and we were on with structural design and investigating envelope options, often requiring more visits to Broadcasting House (the refurbished Broadcasting House and the new Egton wing were opened by The Queen on 20 April 2006 as part of her 80th birthday celebrations) and Lend Lease were well on with Phase 2 which was planned for a 2010 completion. It would be fair to say there was a healthy rivalry between Lend Lease staff delivering the BBC's new buildings at this point, whether in Glasgow, London or Salford, it resulted in an abundance of in-house technical expertise that was only a telephone call away, day or night.

As we came closer to design freeze, the thornier issue of lease negotiations between Peel and the BBC began to emerge. My feeling was that Peel were surprised at the onerous commissioning requirements laid down by their future tenants. I had to make sure that everything was back-to-back with our management contract, risk analysis of this internally was important, as was comparing our agreements on other BBC projects. The excessive number of commissioning phases, seven alone on the BBC Philharmonic studio, was one of the key sticking points prior to the lease being signed off, sensibly we understood that the program could be in jeopardy if the BBC had their way, again it seemed that good relationships built up allowed for an element of compromise on each side. We settled on five.

The BBC signed the Head Lease on 18 May 2007, and we set to work on site clearance. The team then expanded rapidly from half a dozen or so, to around 120 site based staff at peak by the end of 2008. A clear risk at this stage was the 'watering down' of single-minded goals that was easy to achieve in a small group, much less so in an extended team with dozens of packages being designed, procured and delivered across the 15 ha site. It was a test of Lend Lease's rigorous internal quality procedures which won through, tireless co-ordination and tolerance checking, a real commitment to be *'best in class'*. Chris Kane described the performance of Lend Lease at this time as *'exemplary'*. (ibid)

In summary, I believe the following were key contributors to the success of this project:

- Excellent collaboration at design 'concept' stage between the BBC, Developer (Peel) and contractor (Lend Lease), which de-risked misinterpretation and set quality and performance expectations at a very early stage.
- Regular design briefings and site visits organised by the BBC established a 'mindset' of what we as a group wanted to achieve, and provided a real 'bond' and common ground on which respective team members did not feel anxious about proposing novel or radical ideas.
- Familiarisation visits of BBC staff to Mediacity during construction offered the opportunity for both developer and contractor to hear end-user opinions well before handover. This was particularly important to the BBC production staff who were essentially using the new buildings interiors and views out as a backdrop.
- Long term relationships fostered between BBC/Lend Lease – alignment of values, technical understanding over many key projects and knowledge sharing amongst Lend Lease staff.

I am extremely proud of the success of Mediacity and the part I played in its creation. The old adage of *'the more you put in, the more you get out'* was never truer than on this project. After 30 years in the business now, I am convinced that a good bond with fellow team members enhances collective performance dramatically. Having that relationship and back-up always reduces the fear of hard-to-understand technical issues, and inspires confidence in dealing with the inevitable raft of problems that surface on every job.

Biography - Stephen Warburton

Trained as an architect in Oxford and London, Stephen moved to Hong Kong in the mid 90's to pursue a career with development companies. After a prior architectural internship in Washington DC and New York, Stephen was keen to work overseas again, engaged on a diverse range of projects from discrete luxury villas in Nha Trang, Vietnam, to Hong Kong's vast international airport at Chek Lap Kok. On returning to the UK he led Lend Lease's design teams on the BBC's Mediacity project. Still a keen exponent of design in the built environment, he has also tutored students at Oxford School of Architecture, and has had projects exhibited at the Ashmolean Museum in Oxford, which were subsequently published in A Treasury of Graphic Techniques by Tom Porter.

QUALIFICATIONS
- BA (Hons) in Architecture. Oxford Brookes University
- Post-Graduate Diploma in Architecture. Oxford Brookes University
- MSc Construction Economics & Management. London South Bank University
- Chartered Member of the Royal Institute of British Architects

Royal Women's Hospital Melbourne
– The Mechanics of PPP Success

By Graham Whitson B.E (Civil) CBA MAppFin
Managing Director, Bilfinger RE Asset Management (Australia)

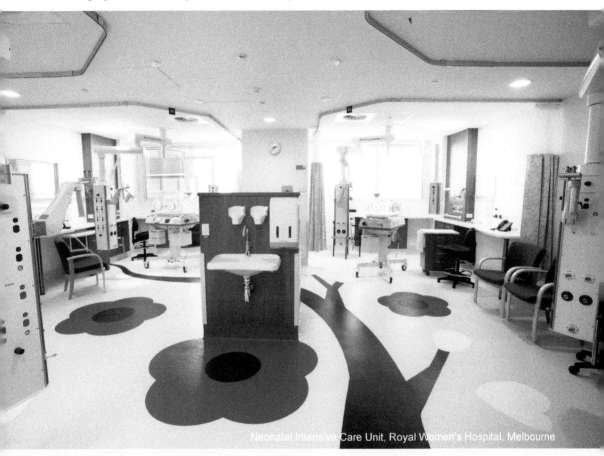

Neonatal Intensive Care Unit, Royal Women's Hospital, Melbourne

A wise Project Manager once explained to me the concept of the 6 P's.

Proper Planning Prevents Piss Poor Performance

Whilst I found this acronym quite amusing at the time, I didn't really think of it again until I became strongly involved in PPP projects. The concept of the 6 P's is very sound. Plan ahead and you can foresee and avoid so many of the problems that have affected construction projects for many years. The use of the 6 P's acronym got me thinking about PPPs and what the P's really stand for.

<u>Public Private Partnerships</u>

They could be described as a partnership between public and private organisations where responsibility for each element of project delivery is assigned to the party who is most capable or competent to manage that element. This is a sound concept also, but the description does not give enough consideration to the "partnership" P of PPPs. After all, the success of a project delivery relies on all components of the project working together harmoniously, not merely assigned or delegated correctly.

PPPs bring a range of stakeholders together to participate in a meaningful and constructive manner to deliver a project. As we are aware, not all projects have been as successful as they could have been. Many projects with a diverse range of stakeholders falter and stumble because the different parties have not come to an agreement on their respective roles, are not clear on their individual expectations and have not agreed on how the relationships between them need to operate.

Like a car, you can't throw all of the components under the bonnet and expect it to work. You must ensure that they are assembled in such a manner that they work effectively together to provide the required outcome. A project team is little different. We must first establish what outcome we want to achieve, assess the components that are needed to get there, then devise how those components can best operate together to achieve that outcome.

The Royal Women's Hospital (RWH) project in Melbourne, Australia, is a good example of how, when a diverse range of stakeholders are brought together, success can be achieved for all parties provided that all stakeholders have a common understanding of the objectives and they work together in a collaborative manner to achieve those objectives.

The mechanics of such a PPP success are as follows:

DESTINATION

On any project, it is necessary to set the destination – where do we want to go? The process to set direction and agreement, especially at a high level, around roles, expectations and relationships can help minimise, if not eliminate, the potential problems that can occur in large project teams.

It is necessary to ensure that all stakeholders on a project are aligned and agreed on how to move forward to produce and deliver a successful project for all stakeholders. We must therefore understand what constitutes success for each stakeholder so that we can create a consistent understanding of each stakeholder's expectations and goals for the project.

Through understanding each stakeholder's 'outcomes for success', we are better equipped to understand our partner's motivations for behaviour and can more easily foresee how they might react in a particular circumstance. The skill of being able to *"put oneself in another's shoes"* is a key to knowing your partners and establishing and maintaining a great project partnership.

COMPONENTS

The suite of stakeholder components in large PPP projects is generally common between one project and the next. You will have a government client, end users, D&C Contractor, FM Contractor, financiers (Debt and Equity), various consultants and independent certifiers. But what are the key ingredients that are needed for a successful team?

The human elements of a project team are the key to its success. PPP's span over long periods of time, making the selection of the right people and the establishment of strong, lasting relationships all the more important. Poor relationships can be difficult to recover so getting off to the right start is critical. The attributes of the project leaders which made the relationships on RWH project so strong can be summarised as follows:

- Strong Leaders – confident decision makers and comfortable speaking to large audiences.
- Excellent Communicators – good at assessing a situation and providing a succinct summary of information, willing to be open and share information.
- Extrovert personalities – will go out of the way to speak with all project team members, not just those at a senior level. Participate in team social events.

- Sound Commercial competency and educated in PPP contracts – not reliant on external legal advice. They must have the confidence to make judgements themselves, knowing that contracts can be interpreted by the reader in many different ways, and that lawyers, in their own self-interest, will typically always give you advice to support your commercial position rather than a balanced view.
- Good mediators – they are able to put themselves in others' shoes, are willing to listen, empathise, and realise that there are two sides to every story.

In addition to having the right leaders for the project, it is important to set the climate for the other team members to perform. Experience shows that a set of guiding behaviours provides a framework upon which the project team can be measured. At RWH, we agreed the behaviours under which we would perform as follows:

We will

- Communicate openly and honestly (say in public what we say in private)
- Work together to achieve our core purpose
- Listen respectfully, seek solutions, understand others' positions and recognize contribution
- Act to encourage and create great solutions and excellent outcomes
- Act fairly and ethically
- Talk first and write later (there will be no surprises)
- Maintain a sense of perspective and humour
- And as a result, enjoy the ride

These behaviours, when displayed on the walls of the various project offices, act as a constant reminder and a measure of accountability throughout the project life. As you will note, many of these are communication based. Many projects suffer as a result of miscommunication or misinterpretation. It is possible for several people to read the same piece of correspondence and arrive at several different interpretations. The behaviour, *"talk first and write later"*, is one way of avoiding these situations by discussing the intent of your correspondence prior to issuing it, that way ensuring that it cannot be misunderstood.

These are the desired human elements of a successful project. The right people and the right behaviours make a difference. Selection of the right people will help lead the team, steer direction, guide behaviours and monitor the controls to ensure the project's destination is reached.

ASSEMBLY

For anything to work well, it must first be assembled correctly. To do this, we must understand what each part of the project team does and how it relates to each other part.

There are two steps in this process

1. Identify the roles and responsibilities of each stakeholder – The purpose of this exercise is to confirm that each stakeholder understands their role, but equally importantly, that other members of the team also understand what the other stakeholders are required to do. This will help highlight the interdependencies, ensure that there is no overlap in task responsibilities, and identify any gaps in the team to be filled.
2. Identify interfaces and interdependencies – It is important to understand the impact your role can have on others in the team. Problems can arise if parts of the team work in isolation and are not inclusive of the ultimate beneficiaries of their work. Knowing the end user of your work will enable communication to develop early and will ensure that the best outcome can be achieved.

These outcomes are best achieved in an open workshop environment, where each stakeholder is invited to present to the collective team their key accountabilities and relationships. The intent is to develop a common understanding of what each of the components of the team will do, and how the interface must work between each stakeholder. This is particularly important in PPPs where a large number of stakeholders are brought together to deliver a project.

FUEL

Not only must the components be assembled correctly to work in a functional manner, they must also have the right fuel to perform. In the project team context, incentives and motivation provide the fuel for performance.

Whilst each of the stakeholders will have their own specific motivations for their participation in the project, it is important to establish a common objective to which all stakeholders can subscribe. This core purpose is an overarching vision or statement of commitment and intent to help stakeholders in their decision making. It is aligned with their goals and in no way impinges on the rights of any of the individual stakeholders.

On the RWH project, we uncovered a very powerful tool to motivate the collective team. It came in the form of a video produced by the hospital, which told the emotional stories of many women who had needed the help of the Women's hospital. The RWH in Melbourne is Australia's largest specialist hospital dedicated to improving the health of women and new born babies. The video had a significant impact on the project team, as many of the people involved could relate these stories to their own family members. It helped the project team grasp the significance of what it was building. It wasn't just bricks and mortar. It was a service that helped people in need, people less fortunate than many of us. This became a very important backdrop for many of the decisions that were later made in relation to the design and functionality of the new facility.

The Core Purpose agreed for the RWH project was to

"Create a sustainable world class healthcare environment that meets the need of women and babies for generations and engenders a sense of pride in all"

Whilst there is nothing particularly incentivising about this statement itself, being displayed on the walls of the various project offices reminded the project team of the video and the significance of the decisions they had to make each day.

EFFICIENCY

Once the team has been assembled, coordinated and has the right incentives to perform, it is important to identify the tools and systems that will help the team perform at its best and achieve the desired outcomes.

The participants in the project are best placed to develop these. Many of them bring good experience from past projects of things that have worked, and others that have not. It is important that the lessons of the past are shared and foster improvement for the future. Again, this is something that can be achieved in an open workshop environment.

Some examples of tools and systems that enhance performance are:

- Meetings structure and schedule – PPP projects involve multiple stakeholders and large teams operating at varying levels of responsibility or technical competency. A regular timetable of meetings is necessary to avoid the laborious and inefficient task of coordinating multiple diaries and schedules. It is necessary to have a meetings structure in place which

    - Facilitates strong communication across the project team
    - Cascades responsibilities at varying levels, and promotes escalation of issues to a higher level for resolution
    - Covers the entire suite of meetings needs across the project

It is always difficult to get multiple stakeholders in the same place at the same time. It is therefore essential to have a meetings schedule in place which

- Provides fixed meetings days and times for specific meetings, and appropriate durations
- Contains information relating to location, attendees and responsibility for the chair and minutes
- Encourages the various project stakeholders to conduct their internal meetings in common timeslots, thus maximising common availability at other times
- Provides unallocated meetings slots common to all parties diaries that can be used in the event of unexpected meetings requirements.

It is also advisable to insist on instant minutes from all project meetings. These need only be hand written, but should be

▶ Discussed at the end of the meeting to confirm a consistent understanding of the actions and outcomes agreed in the meeting

▶ Disseminated immediately following the meeting to ensure that action is taken immediately and is not delayed

- Communication Protocols – Given the large quantity of people involved in such projects, it is imperative that information is received by the person who most needs it. The establishment of clear guidelines for dissemination of information is a must.

- Collaboration systems – In conjunction with the Communications protocols, a web based collaboration system is recommended to ensure the efficient transfer and storage of correspondence and documents between the respective project parties.

- Reporting structures – Establish a clear set of expectations in terms of reporting content, distribution, frequency and quality.

- Escalation Procedures – Establish clear mechanisms to encourage the project team to identify and escalate issues in a timely manner so that they can be resolved quickly and mitigate any impact of delay or frustration. A senior leadership team can be established outside of the contract framework to discuss such manners without prejudice and agree actions to resolve such matters.

MAINTENANCE

Whilst an open workshop early in the project is the ideal way to establish a well-functioning and committed project team from the outset, it is essential to review performance on a regular basis and assess areas for improvement.

A second workshop one year into the project provides a good opportunity to:

- Recap on the ground covered in the first workshop (particularly for those people new to the project)
- Refresh what makes a successful team – communication, flexibility, willingness to listen and understand each parties' concerns
- Assess progress toward the team's core purpose – what has the team done to support achievement of the core purpose?
- Reiterate the agreed behaviours for the team to follow
- Review the systems and processes that were established to enable the project to be successful, assess their value and identify how the team can improve further.

The RWH Project was a well-oiled machine that delivered PPP success. It was not achieved by accident, or through generous programs, clear skies and comfortable pricing. It was achieved through the establishment of an efficient, well synchronised project delivery team who understood their roles and were committed to a common outcome.

Achievements:

- A responsive, flexible and open consultation process with the hospital and end users that led to over 600 functional design changes and optimal selection of equipment at no additional cost. The result has been the highest levels of client satisfaction and a building relevant to its communities.
- No outstanding claims or disputes, and a broad based commitment to partnering and team work that delivered the project on time, on budget, with the minimum of fuss
- Regular weekly stakeholder meetings and six monthly strategic workshops with partners kept the project on track to handover, while ongoing smooth relations will ensure its operational maintenance over 25 years
- Constant consultation and thorough training with hospital staff provided for a seamless transition into the new facility and high degree of user satisfaction
- Achieved steady state operations within 12 months of completion, including rectification of all defects
- Sound operational performance over 6 years
- Profitable to all private sector participants
- Strong project relationships to this day

The mechanics of PPPs are simple, but can be very effective when properly constructed.

Biography – Graham Whitson

Graham started his career with Leighton Contractors and worked on numerous major construction projects within Australia in a Project Management capacity over 13 years (1992 to 2005). These projects included Melbourne's Western Ring Road, the Jolimont Rail Yard rationalisation (Federation Square), Optus and Nextgen Fibre Optic cable networks and the Spencer Street Station Redevelopment(or Southern Cross Station) – his first PPP project.

Graham joined Bilfinger in 2005 as the Project Director of the Special Purpose Company responsible for the Royal Women's Hospital Redevelopment. He became Executive Director, Operations at Bilfinger in 2008, and was more recently appointed Managing Director of Bilfinger's Australian business following the restructure of its concessions business.

Graham has worked in the PPP space for 12 years, with direct delivery experience on 6 PPPs and bid involvement on more than a dozen PPPs. Delivered projects include Southern Cross Station, Victoria Prisons (MCC and MRC), Royal Women's Hospital, Ararat Prison, Peninsula Link, and the Northern Territory Secure Facilities Project (Darwin Prison).

London 2012 Olympic & Paralympic Games – Securing Success

By Ian Williams MSc, CEng, FICE, FCIArb
Former Head of Projects for the Government Olympic Executive, London 2012
Executive Manager for the Supreme Committee for the Qatar 2022 World Cup

London Olympic Park

Success for the London 2012 Olympics could be measured in many ways, such as the sell-out of the tickets; the quality of the sport; the transport operations met all demands; and the security operation ensured no incidents affected the Games. All commentators, without exception, heralded the 2012 London Olympic and Paralympic Games as a great success. Ultimately the summer of spectacular sport and how London performed as a city is what most people remember. However, behind the sport was approximately seven years of preparation covering the construction of Olympic Park and its competition and non-competition venues. This preparation was the foundation for regeneration of East London, the transport and security operations, the public services and the planning and execution of the Games. The National Audit Office (the independent UK government body scrutinizing public spending) stated in their Post Games Review Report that *'The successful staging of the Olympics has been widely acknowledged.' ....and... 'By any reasonable measure the Games were a success and the big picture is that they delivered value for money'.*

This paper covers the factors that led to the success of the activities that were funded by a £9.3 billion pounds public sector package, with the building and commissioning of the Olympic Park and its venues making up about 75% of the budget.

Olympic Park covered about 250 hectares of what would be in legacy a new urban Park, which has about 100 hectares of open space and which created one of Europe's largest urban parks for 150 years. Over 200 buildings were demolished and 98% of the demolition materials were used or recycled; using five soil-washing machines about 80% (1.4 million cubic metres) of contaminated soil was cleaned and reused. The Olympic Park included several permanent and temporary venues; the 80,000 seat Olympic Stadium and warm up track; 17,000 seat Aquatics centre; the Water Polo arena; 6,000 seat Velodrome; 12,000 seat Basketball arena; the Hockey arena; 7,000 seat Handball arena; Paralympic Tennis centre; the International Broadcasting and Media Centres; and last but not least the 3,600 bed Athletes' Village.

Whilst the construction risks in themselves were challenging, the major risk identified at the outset was the ability of government to deliver infrastructure within the allocated budget and to an immovable deadline. In 2005, on the announcement that London was the successful city, the immovable deadline of the 26th June 2012 for the opening ceremony was fixed. In 2007, it was identified that the main areas of risk that needed to be addressed were the need for strong governance and delivery structures given the multiplicity of organisations and groups involved; the need for a budget to be clearly determined and managed, applying effective procurement measures; the need for effective progress monitoring and risk management arrangements; and above all people with the right skills to deliver.

At the outset, the government appointed a specialist recruitment consultant to source key individuals with proven major project experience and expertise in commercial and financial aspects of major projects. A number of key characteristics were sought; a clear understanding of the balance between value and cost, and individuals with a 'can do' attitude who were resourceful, who would find solutions and were collaborative in their approach.

It was planned to hand over the control of Olympic Park and the Athletes' Village in early 2012 to the London Organising Committee of the Olympic Games and Paralympic Games (LOCOG) and it was formed to act as the principal organisation for the Games. Many of the venues on the Park had already been handed over to them ahead of time and test events held in advance.

In construction terms, achievements on the Olympic Park were extraordinary and had placed the British construction industry at the forefront of delivering major projects. The Park was delivered to schedule and within budget, with the anticipated out-turn cost of the Park, infrastructure and the Village at £7.2 billion.

London 2012 did not escape the credit crunch. In 2008 the Athletes' Village PFI (PPP) deal collapsed and the government had no alternative option but to fund its construction. However, evidence of the attractiveness of the regeneration and the strong commercial demand for the Olympic assets in legacy mode has since been demonstrated by the deal with Delancey and Qatari Diar for the Athletes' Village.

Governance – A single government department was made responsible for the leadership of the public sector funding package, the Department for Culture, Media and Sport through its Government Olympic Executive (GOE). To supplement the team, the GOE recruited a small number of individuals for key roles with a proven track record of experience in delivering major projects. A delivery body, the Olympic Delivery Authority (ODA) was set-up to deliver the infrastructure and venues. ODA was the contracting authority and appointed a delivery partner (CLM) to manage and administer the procurement and the delivery of works contracts. The key for both organisations was ensuring the right skills-sets corporately and individually.

Significantly, GOE was given authority to put in place a governance structure and processes which applied adequate formality to decision making and funding control while maintaining short decision-making timetables. The forum for key decisions and funding decisions and the release of funding was the Olympic Program Review Group (OPRG), which was made up of representatives from the government funding and public body funding organisations, chaired by GOE. OPRG reviewed monthly schedule and cost positions and applied clear procedures for release of contingency funds, leading eventually to Ministerial approval. Regular reporting and review ensured that cost management, risk management and management of the limited contingency fund were aligned.

In 2008, GOE pulled together a comprehensive and realistic budget for the Olympics, which included a contingency element. This budget was articulated in a readily available document, which also outlined the scope, scope ownership and time element for each element of the program. On agreement of the budget, the GOE was given the authority to manage the release and spending of the budget under the governance of OPRG. This enabled fast decision-making acknowledging the immovable deadline of the Olympics. Through its effectiveness, OPRG gained the confidence of government funding departments which was the key to the decision-making process. Release of funding for projects was based on submission of business cases. Once approved, the ODA were given authority to manage the budget release and had delegated authority for release of contingency funds.

In response to the governance structure put in place, the ODA applied effective procurement measures to all the projects. They developed a transparent procurement code using the New Engineering Contract V3 (NEC 3) standard form of contract. The adoption of the NEC 'cost-reimbursed' form of contract in the main was the key to ensuring flexibility and agility to overcome challenges presented by the project delivery. Acknowledging the disruptive nature of protracted disputes, the procurement code outlined a three-tier dispute avoidance & resolution process, which involved setting up an Independent Dispute Avoidance Panel (IDAP), a dedicated Adjudication Panel, with the final tribunal being the Technology & Construction Court.

At the outset effective progress monitoring and risk management arrangements were considered critical tools to manage the Olympics program. Coupled with the use of 'cost-reimbursed' contracts, transparency of facts was the foundation that supported the governance structure and the timely decision making that was so necessary. This transparency through reporting was also made available to the public on a quarterly basis. This had a powerful effect of demonstrating a 'no surprise' approach and the opportunity for public scrutiny from which public confidence in the delivery of the Program was to evolve. Managing risk was put central to the decision-making process, with regular evaluation and adjustments made to the measures needed to minimise or ideally eliminate risks.

The final key success factor was having people with the right skills to deliver throughout all the organisations. The Government acknowledged that it needed to act and perform as an 'intelligent' but lean client organisation. To this end, it recruited individuals from the private sector with a proven track record in delivering major projects. The fundamental shift that also occurred from traditional government procurement was the delegation and authority given to the individuals to ensure delivery to the budget and timescales within the governance process specifically developed for the Olympics.

In summary, the success of Olympic Park and the Games was underpinned by using a purpose-built delivery model with governance clarity. Central to this was the dedicated GOE team, led by specially recruited staff. The delivery organisations also recruited specialist individuals. For senior roles, acknowledgement of remuneration packages above background levels was necessary to attract the appropriate individuals with the right focus and behaviours. The challenge of an immovable deadline, whilst posing a significant challenge, also presented delivery opportunities which supported the need for timely decision making processes and delegation of authority to the appropriate people at the right levels in the organisations, because these people best understood the risks and the actions needed to manage these risks and to make the right decisions to meet the budget and time challenges. The model adopted allowed the ODA to realise savings and for GOE to redistribute funds to cover other areas of risk pressures that developed in the operational readiness phase of the Olympics, such as the well-documented security staff aspects. The approach adopted by the UK Government is a testament to the boldness of the Government in changing its approach, with the result being world-acclaimed success.

All organisations were aligned to a common goal and the leadership came together regularly to evaluate progress and resolve issues. The common goal fostered a culture that meant there was only one possible outcome - hosting a successful Olympic Games. This ethos resulted in everyone associated with the program taking personal responsibility and pride in their part in working towards that goal. Flowing from this were positive attitudes that all issues needed to be resolved in a timely way. This was very evident in the final twelve months of preparation for the Games, when interfaces were at the most crucial stage. GOE allocated a substantial element of contingency in order to resolve issues rapidly and coupled with this was specific delegation to a group to administer the budget on behalf of the Minister for the Olympics. This group dealt with up to 30 issues on a weekly basis making sound but rapid decisions which resulted in solutions being quickly implemented and excellent working relationships being maintained and even strengthened. This process continued into the operation of the Games and proved effective and contributed to the incident free aspect of the Games.

In conclusion, whilst the government and the supporting organisations set-up sound, practical governance and processes, the underlying factor was having the right people, with the right behaviours, doing the right thing at the right time.

Reference – National Audit Office, The London 2012 Olympic Games and Paralympic Games: post Games review, HC 794, session 2012-13, 5th December 2012.

Biography – Ian Williams

Ian is a Chartered Engineer and a Fellow of the Institution of Civil Engineers and Institute of Arbitrators. He has 25 years' experience in major engineering projects in the UK, Southern Africa, the Middle East and South East Asia. Ian is currently responsible for infrastructure and transport aspects for the Qatar 2022 World Cup for the Supreme Committee. Before joining the Supreme Committee, he was Head of Projects for the Government Olympic Executive on the London 2012 Olympic Games. Prior to the Olympics, he held key positions on the delivery of metros in London and Singapore, and airport infrastructure developments at Heathrow for Terminal 5 and the redevelopment of Terminals 3 & 4.

Risky Business: the Exceptional Sydney Opera House

By Dr Anne Watson (BA (Hons), MA, PhD)
Author of "Building a Masterpiece: the Sydney Opera House" (2006/2013)

In October 2013 the Sydney Opera House celebrated its 40th anniversary. It was an occasion for much reminiscing about the building's troubled gestation during the 1960s, but also its unprecedented success as an internationally regarded architectural and cultural icon. Amongst the predictably wide media coverage of the festivities was an article announcing that, according to a recent study by Deloitte Access Economics, the dollar value of the Opera House could now be estimated at a staggering $4.6 billion.[1] The article noted that the building, which cost $102 million at its completion in 1973, would cost $823 million to rebuild today and that the total value of the built asset was $2.3 billion. The remaining $2.3 billion was calculated as the Opera House's 'intangible' worth over the next 40 years – revenue from tourism, performances, job creation and that most intangible asset of all, the 'iconic' brand status of the building as an immediately recognisable national symbol. The article concluded on a buoyant note, quoting the report's claim that the Opera House could *'help Australia shape its broader economic destiny'!* Meaningless spin – or a corporate strategy to attract the $1 billion necessary for the proposed Opera House renewal program – the article's hype nonetheless underlines the extraordinary pulling power of this world-renowned symbol of a country not otherwise known for its architectural heritage.

---

[1] Rick Feneley, 'We Got it for a Song but its Value has Soared', Sydney Morning Herald, 17 October 2013.

Yet in risk management terms the Opera House broke every rule in the book: a cost escalation of 1400 percent, a ten-year completion delay, political misrepresentation and manipulation, client mismanagement, interpersonal conflict and, most dire of all, the resignation of the architect well before completion. The story of the building's epic design and construction has been likened to the drama of grand opera – and it was.

Sydney's Opera House was the result of an international competition conducted by the New South Wales Labor government in 1956. With hindsight it is obvious the competition brief, developed in consultation with the Royal Australian Institute of Architects, was over-optimistic in terms of the seating quotas identified for the two main halls and, most significantly, in its stipulation of a dual-purpose main hall combining concerts and opera. Many of the prospective competition entrants queried the wisdom of a hall uniting facilities for two performance genres with very different seating, staging and acoustic requirements and, indeed, the difficulty of resolving these conflicting constraints substantially contributed to the impasse the project reached in 1965.

As is well-known, the competition was won by the young, some might say inexperienced, Danish architect Jørn Utzon (1918-2008) on the basis of his relatively schematic drawings for those freeform sculptural curves that were immediately likened to billowing sails. This was an appealing metaphor for a harbour site, although the responses in the press on the day after the announcement of the winning entry on 29 January 1957 were not always so kind. One wit likened Utzon's design to looking like a 'disintegrating circus tent in a gale' and another thought it looked like a 'piece of Danish pastry'! It was day one of the constant media attention the Opera House would receive over the next 15 or so years. Most newspapers carried images, not of Utzon's drawings, but of the perspective hastily prepared by the Sydney modernist architect Arthur Baldwinson at the request of the judges: Utzon's only perspective showed a small view of part of the staircase between the two halls. And while the four judges were all enthusiastic about the daring of the winning scheme it is worth noting that three of them initially rejected Utzon's entry: it was American architect Eero Saarinen, arriving late for the judging, who rescued Utzon's drawings from the reject pile and convinced the other three that this was the building that Sydney had to have. Utzon's unique scheme was also unusual in that it placed the halls side by side, not back to back, on the relatively narrow Bennelong Point site, thus sowing the seeds for the problems later encountered over inadequate seating numbers and the narrow stage areas. The cost of the building was initially estimated at £3.5 million (AUD$7 million).

Saarinen, himself a prominent enthusiast for the possibilities of shell concrete, may have held sway but it is likely that one of the reasons for the other judges initially rejecting Utzon's scheme was that it was light on for technical, particularly structural, detail – a fact no doubt noticed by the irrepressible Ove Arup (1895-1988) who was on the phone offering his services to Utzon only days after the competition winner was announced. Still engaged as the Opera House structural engineering consultants today, Arup's global reputation has been substantially reinforced by the company's long association with the building. Perseverance may well have been one of the firm's most valuable assets because it would take three years of close collaboration with Utzon – and pioneering computer programming – before the geometry and construction principles for the shells were resolved. During this time the 'sails' evolved from Utzon's mathematically undefinable curves through ten different roof schemes to the final spherical solution articulated in Utzon's 'Yellow Book' in early 1962.

In the meantime – and despite the evolving nature of the design – construction of the foundations had commenced in early March 1959, due to the urgings of Labor Premier Joe Cahill, one of the initiators of the Opera House project in the mid-1950s. Fearing that a loss at the forthcoming state elections on 21 March would stymy the project, Cahill had released premature and unrealistically low budget figures - £4.88 million in April 1958 – before any working drawings were available, and was fast-tracking construction as a political expediency. In their article *'Delusion and Deception in Large Infrastructure Projects',*[2] the authors cite this lack of candour at the very start of the project as the source of many later problems, but the corollary to this is that had anything approaching the

---

[2]Bent Flyvberg, Massimo Garbuio, Dan Lovallo, 'Delusion and Deception in Large Infrastructure Projects', California Management Review, vol 51, no 2, Winter 2009, p 178.

real cost and construction duration and difficulties been known, the project would never have been started. So, ironically, in many ways it was due to Premier Cahill's political manoeuvring that the Opera House was eventually realised. While the Labor party was narrowly re-elected, Cahill would not live to see Stage 1 of the building, the construction of the podium, emerge from the rubble of Bennelong Point. Aged 68, he died in October 1959.

One of Cahill's legacies was the Opera House lottery set up to fund construction of the building. Despite galloping cost estimates - £24.77 million ($50 million) in mid-1965, $85 million in September 1968 – and constantly revised opening dates, the lotteries were successful in meeting most of the final $102 million expenditure. Thus while the selection of the unprecedented Opera House design was itself a huge gamble, its realisation was also made possible from the proceeds of gambling.

Any gamble is not without risk and one of the several human casualties of the great Opera House speculative venture was, of course, Utzon. The downward spiral of Utzon's relationship with his consultants, particularly Arup's, and the government from 1963 when he relocated from Denmark to Sydney, to his resignation on 28 February 1966 has been well documented. At the heart of the multitude of problems that led to the final denouement was the disconnect between Utzon's perfectionism and inability to compromise, the complex functional requirements of the building and the politically expedient need to complete the building and to rein in costs. Almost ten years after the competition, these conflicting ingredients were a recipe for disaster.

Utzon was one of the victims of the great Opera House gamble and so in many ways was his successor, Peter Hall (1931-1995). A rising star in the Sydney architecture community, Hall was the design architect in the consortium, Hall Todd & Littlemore, set up to complete what Utzon had left behind, principally the design of all the interiors, the paving and cladding of the building and the glass walls enclosing it. In a project beset by controversy, perhaps the greatest of them all was the dispute engendered by Hall – and the government's – decision in early 1967 to redesign the main hall as a single purpose concert hall and to transfer opera and ballet to what had been originally designated a drama theatre. In the process Utzon's daring, but technically untested ideas for using huge plywood sheets for the ceilings of the halls were reluctantly abandoned, as was his controversial plywood mullion scheme for the glass walls. Hall's recommendations, informed by close study of overseas precedents and reference to experienced international consultants, provided the circuit breaker that ended the terrible impasse that was stymying progress in early 1966, and ultimately provided Sydney with a functioning, much-loved performance venue. But Hall was never to escape the opprobrium of many of his colleagues for abandoning Utzon's designs, nor the looming presence of the world-famous building on Bennelong Point. Never to fulfil the promise of his early achievements, Hall's financial problems, a stagnating career and a fairly chaotic personal life contributed to his early death aged 64 in 1995. In most histories of the Opera House the work of Hall and his team is, sadly, either denigrated or completely overlooked.

The term 'risk management' is a relatively modern one in the construction industry. Structured risk management processes were not widely used in the early 1960s. Arguably, had a framework for managing risk been applied to the Opera House it would never have gotten off the ground.

Yet for all the drama and conflict of its evolution – the very human failings that dogged its progress – it has been an unprecedented success; as a tourist destination, a popular performance venue for audiences and an inspirational one for many performers. Once described by Utzon as being at the *'edge of the possible'*, the technologies developed to overcome the building's major technical hurdles have also had important consequences for the construction industry. Far from a disaster, the Opera House has been a spectacular triumph. **This book quite correctly proposes that 'erroneous human behaviour' is the cause of most major project debacles, but it also begs the question as to why the Opera House is such a remarkable exception. I would suggest that it was the challenge of the creative brilliance of Utzon's scheme that, against all odds, motivated and inspired all those connected with the building's long and difficult gestation.**

Just as human dynamics frustrated the building's progress so sheer human persistence and ingenuity ensured its completion. After his resignation Utzon remarked to the Minister for Public Works, Davis Hughes, that 'It is not I but Sydney Opera House that creates all the enormous difficulties'.[3] He was partially correct for it was the audacious but fundamentally conceptual nature of his competition scheme that set the project on an uncertain and unknowable journey into the future. **All great human achievements involve great risk: the Opera House was no exception.**

Acknowledgment May 2014 - *With thanks to Jim Anderson, architect and head of the Hall Todd & Littlemore glass walls team for the Sydney Opera House 1967-69, for providing the opportunity and encouragement to contribute this essay.*

---

[3]Correspondence, Jørn Utzon to Davis Hughes, 15 March 1966.

Biography – Dr Anne Watson

Dr Anne Watson recently completed a PhD thesis (Sydney University) on Peter Hall's work at the Sydney Opera House 1966-70. She was formerly curator of architecture and design at the Powerhouse Museum, Sydney where her interest in the history of the Opera House developed through research for an exhibition and book, Building a Masterpiece: the Sydney Opera House, in 2006. Since then she has written extensively and curated several exhibitions on the Opera House. Currently she is an independent curator and writer and is editor and contributing author of a book exploring the residential designs of Walter Burley Griffin and Marion Mahony Griffin in suburban Sydney in the 1920s and 30s.

Unintended 'human risk' consequences from the Sydney Opera House

There is a further interesting 'human factors' risk management story to be told about the Sydney Opera House project (which is equally applicable to other similar challenging projects).

Sourcing an economic fixed-price construction commitment is often very difficult in projects which have unique and/or incomplete design briefs. Main Contractors tend to price for all of these uncertainties, and the Client often ends up with the offer of a lump-sum construction contract which is way over the constraints of the available budget. A common solution to this (as happened in the construction of Sydney Opera House) is for the Contractor to be engaged on a 'cost-plus' basis. This provides a cheaper initial price, but the Client then assumes most of the risk of any additional costs arising from the changes to design and construction methods as the project progresses – surely a big win for the Contractor?

Well, not always so! The Contractor's approach to dealing with a 'lump-sum' or a 'cost-plus' project will usually be very different, and their team will have to adapt their style to suit accordingly. If a Contractor has long-term involvement in a major 'cost-plus' style contract, they need to be very careful in what happens with their risk management style and procedures at the end of that period. In the specific case of the Opera House, the Main Contractor was almost consumed by the challenges of this single project for nearly 10 years. However, in the five years following completion, the Contractor then proceeded to lose much of the value that they had gained in the 10 years of working at 'cost-plus'. The reason for this is primarily one of human risk management, after 10 years of 'cost-plus' working, the Contractor organisation had lost many of the risk appraisal and management skills that were needed to properly price and manage 'normal' projects on a lump-sum basis.

The lesson from this, and similar stories – risk management requirements are constantly evolving. What worked for the projects we dealt with last year may not actually be applicable to the risk profile we have to manage today. We need to constantly monitor and upgrade our understanding of the risks we are trying to manage – and then ensure that our key personnel are trained and supported in managing an evolving situation.

Common Causes of Project Failure

In the following pages we have identified 20 common causes of failure arising from actions taken during the creation of a project, the tendering, bidding and pre-contract phase of projects and 15 post-contract ones arising during detailed design, construction, commissioning and transition to operations. All these causes of failure are related to shortcomings in management in one way or another and always involve human inputs. These shortcomings are mostly at senior level with the principle stakeholders; including the client, the bid team, design consultants, project and construction managers and services contractors. The common element is invariably the human input and not the technical processes.

In order to be fair and objective we first need to clarify just what is 'project failure' and why do projects fail, keeping in mind that 'failure' is likely to have a different meaning for everyone, depending on your perspective. It can relate to one of the objectives of any party involved in a project not being met. This may include cost, time, client expectation, shareholder or boardroom expectation, safety targets, functionality or fit for purpose, public or political expectations and perceptions, etc.

Generally though, failure is referred to in terms of cost over-runs and program blow-outs for various reasons and these causes of failure are analysed and explained to clients, owners and shareholders ad nauseam.

But why do project failures keep happening? Why can't major international companies, at the very least, develop risk management systems that prevent project failures? We are talking about massive failures, not the marginal losses that often occur in projects which do not put the existence of the whole company at risk.

Projects that fail generally do so for a combination of reasons as well and we analyse these different reasons in depth. However, the one common denominator amongst all these reasons is human behaviour at some stage or other in the process as shown in the following examples.

The global construction and civil engineering industry is notorious for its slim margins, typically in the 2% - 3% range, which are brought about by the competitive bidding process and this leaves no room for mismanagement, but fine margins are not a prime cause of failed projects.

My interest is in finding out why some projects are very successful and why others have catastrophic program overruns and financial losses; cost overruns that can vastly exceed the original contract price.

There have been many projects around the world that are famous (or infamous) for their losses and delays. Two extreme examples are the Sydney Opera House and more recently, the Scottish Parliament Building which had an initially cost estimate of £40-50m and a final cost of £431m
http://www.parliament.uk/briefing-papers/SN03357.pdf

The Sydney Opera House is a magnificent world renowned building that was budgeted to cost $7m in 1959 and be completed by 1963. It ended up costing $102m on completion in 1973, 10 years later than originally planned.
www.en.wikipedia.org/wiki/Sydney_Opera_House

However, the Sydney Opera House is a rare example of a major project that has been so successful as an international icon that the cost and time it took to build have long since been forgotten. It was paid for by a special public lottery so the taxpayers were not able to complain about that. Now in 2014, 40 years after it opened, we are especially privileged to be able to include Chapter 9 on the Opera House, contributed by Dr Anne Watson, who is well recognised as an historian of the Opera House; with acknowledgment and thanks to Jim Anderson, one of the principal architects on the project, for his valuable background information.

With government-backed projects some commentators say that it is not surprising they get out of hand because politicians interfere too much for their own political purposes, don't understand the processes or the risks and don't let the professional public servants run the projects unhindered (shades of *Yes Minister!*)[1]

To an extent this is correct, as demonstrated by the number of high profile government sponsored disasters listed throughout this book, but as a generalisation it is unfair, because there are many government projects around the world that are highly successful, including both traditional D&C projects and PPPs. The most common criticism of government projects is that government authorities have a perennial habit of underestimating the total cost and the program, with figures being bandied about in the order of 20% to 50% for each. Such underestimating is a sure sign of inexperience or incompetence, or even good politics – if you knew the *'real'* out-turn cost projects wouldn't get off the ground. There would not have been a Sydney Opera House!

'Optimism bias' in public sector projects is not uncommon and creates unrealistic expectations by under-estimating time and cost and over-estimating the benefits. Therefore, when governments are looking at taking on innovative projects or ones with a higher risk profile, they should ensure that their investment decisions are based on realistic estimates and assumptions and that they have identified the potential risks as far as possible, with appropriate cost contingencies and mitigation plans.

However, to put things into balance there are many highly professional government authorities around the world that bring complex projects in on time, on budget and to a high standard of quality, with these projects covering civil engineering (roads and bridges, etc.) as well as general construction works.

Many government professional authorities rely heavily on industry professionals to advise them and sometimes this advice has been found wanting in major projects that have run into trouble. Then the blame game starts, with the politicians and bureaucrats saying they were badly advised and the industry professionals saying that their advice wasn't heeded.

But what about major projects that are fully within the control of the contractor, that have been won on a lump sum Bid submitted after all the checks and balances have been applied at all corporate levels, and they then still incur huge losses? There are many examples that show how this can and does happen.

The following is the detailed list of the common causes of project failure that I have identified. These *'common causes'* nearly all occur during the structuring of the project, bidding, design and construction, commissioning and transition to operations, and rarely after the facilities have commenced commercial operations.

I have only provided explanations and examples for the items that I consider most critical and generally the most common causes of failure. Examples of all the items listed would fill a book on their own, but they are not necessary because they are either well understood by readers involved in the industry or they are self-explanatory.

---

[1] *'Yes Minister'* was a popular BBC comedy in the 1980's

Bid and Pre-Contract Phase

1. <u>Rushing into a project without it being properly structured</u>, with inadequate planning and organisation from the start; all too hurried; the tender going out too early; the contract being awarded too early; all before the budgets and financing, design, construction and operational requirements being properly defined. Common to this sort of approach is a lack of a structured management platform and effective controls being put in place. The inevitable result will be increased costs, high claims by the contractor and delays in construction.
See Hamburg Philharmonic Hall, Chapter 21, Planning and Programming

2. <u>Failing to run design development and cost planning in parallel</u>

   Failing to run design development *'hand-in-glove'* with cost planning can lead to very costly errors in D&C projects. This can apply with the schematic design during a D&C bid and also with the detailed design after signing the contract.

   This is an inherent and significant risk in the construction industry's fragmented and non-integrated way of working. On every project, the team faces the eternal question that keeps everyone awake at night, *"How do you know that the costing is keeping up to date with the progress of the design and that the design being put forward will be competitive in price; that everything has been included in the costs and that the estimators know that they have been told everything?"*

   It is fundamental that D&C design development and cost planning run in close parallel so that different design options can be priced immediately and that there is ample opportunity for value engineering, all in the context of the targeted total Bid price that the Bid director will be aiming at. With large projects and tight Bid programs it is a real trap if the design team gets too far ahead of the cost planners, because if it is found that the total Bid price is looking too high and the submission deadline is rapidly closing then there is no time left for the design team to consider other options and has remedy the situation. This is where tight Bid program management becomes have so important.

   After commencing the Contract there is not as much urgency but a lot of time can still be wasted if the detailed design development is not closely monitored for cost against the contract price. Client user groups often see this phase of the design development as an opportunity to get more for their money and the design and cost managers have to be careful to stick to the specifications they offered in the Bid.

3. <u>Failure to properly involve the future facility managers in the design process</u>, both during bidding and in the detailed design development.

   This situation can arise with design and construction projects where there is an obligation on the developer or contractor to provide the client with a facility in a fully operational condition and where the client will be contracting out the facilities management to a specialist FM company, or even when the client is planning to manage the FM themselves, in which case the client needs to participate in the development of the project as if they were an independent facilities manager. For the sake of the exercise, assume that the project will have a 30 year life cycle in the same manner as a PPP.

   The most common cause of problems in this area is <u>not</u> involving the facilities manager early enough and fully enough. When this happens:

   - Design development does not benefit from the expertise of the facilities manager in terms of materials and equipment selection, serviceability and optimum life cycle, e.g. hypothetically, *"granite can be cheaper than bricks in the long term"* or in practical terms, a higher capital cost today for a more efficient system may prove to be the best investment in the long run when daily running costs and life cycle replacement are both considered in the financial modelling.

- The facilities manager will have to accept what they are handed and if it is found down the track that some of the services are difficult and expensive to maintain then they are in no position to complain or try and recover unexpected costs.

- Without this full involvement it is almost certain that items and costs will be missed or there will be poor procurement selections, to the detriment of both the client/user and the facilities manager.

- Additionally, it is likely that the scope of the future services in the FM subcontract will be inadequate and lead to disputes down the track.

The facilities manager therefore needs to be fully involved from the Bid stage, right through D&C and in the completion, commissioning and transition when they take over responsibility.

This is such an important area of risk management that we list the following indicative areas in which the facilities manager should be involved:

Bid Phase
- Technical and operational evaluations
- Selection of building systems, M&E, IT and security systems
- Systems efficiency, maintenance and life cycle implications
- Undertake energy modelling

D & C Phase
- Participation in the design development and user group process
- Participate in the health, safety and environment policies
- Development of policies and operational manuals
- Develop systems for the control and reporting of the services
- Build the asset data base for the facility
- Sign-off all design and procurement

Commissioning and Transition to Operations
- Train and induct the FM and client staff
- Witness all commissioning and testing of building systems
- Create crisis communications and management plans
- Formulate drills for emergency evacuations
- Stock and equip consumable items and maintenance stores
- Ensure Asset Register is accurate and up to date
- Arrange FM/client coordination and communications on a daily basis

The above list is by no means comprehensive, but is intended to alert managers to the areas to be covered generally and the potential risks that will arise if any key areas are overlooked.

4. Insufficient key subcontracts signed up with firm prices before bid submission or signing of the contract

This is really gambling. A contractor can only minimise their cost risk if they have pricing commitments from the majority of their suppliers and subcontractors in accordance with the design and specification and are confident that their cost estimates for those not locked in are conservative and will cover the situation. *Subcontractors are a wily bunch and they will quickly realise if a head contractor is exposed. It is a dead give-away if RFP's are issued after the main contract has been signed, but you will be surprised how many contractors still do it.*

A risk management check in sufficient time before the bidding process is complete should pick this up.

5. <u>Insufficient investigation of key risk areas pre-bid or pre-contract.</u> Ignore at your peril:

- Fire regulations and compliance (make the Fire Regulatory Authority your best friend)
- Health, safety and environmental provisions
- Time and cost involved in commissioning, completion and QA sign-off

There are a number of areas where both Employers and Contractors have been badly caught out on a regular basis over the years:

- Employers because they have not done sufficient investigation of potential risk areas or made adequate allowances in their budget before entering into a contract, or because they have not included adequate terms in the contract for passing on potential risks.

- Contractors that don't have methodical processes can miss expensive items in the rush to submit the Bid, including discrepancies in the contract documents that end up going against them.

6. <u>Insufficient written qualifications in the Bid concerning key risk areas</u> in the contract documents, which include the drawings and specifications.

More often than not bidding is a stressful process and many items are left to be finalised at the last moment, out of necessity. One of the risks arising from this for contractors is that qualifications to the Bid will be overlooked in the final rush to the line. This can cause disputes down the track when the contractor says *"but I didn't allow for this"* and the client responds *"sorry but you did not qualify that in your Bid"*.

With large Bids it is important that there is a designated Risk Manager who takes responsibility for collating all the risk management items and checks with the team leaders of all the other segments of the Bid. *(See Chapter 20 – Corporate Governance and Effective Operational Risk Management – Team Structure Org Chart for Risk Management)*

Qualifications can also work against the client's interest and budget if they are included by the contractor, but the client doesn't readily pick them up.

A simple example from a real project

The contract was for the supply, fabrication and erection of structural steelwork for infrastructures at an Australian coalmine. The tender drawings were obviously incomplete, consisting of basic site layout plans showing the structures required with plan dimensions, schematic elevations showing dimensions and some drawings showing typical member sizes, spans and connections. The tender called on bidders to make allowance for the missing detail, of which there was quite a bit, and submit a lump sum price for the completed works, based on their knowledge of what should be required and answers to questions they were invited to submit.

The contractor submitted a non-compliant bid, clearly stating in the covering letter that their price was for a given tonnage of steel erected, broken down into the categories shown on the enclosed schedule with matching rates and that any tonnage supplied over and above would be charged as extra. The written qualifications were clear and unambiguous.

The final price increased by 20% over the Bid price and the client initially refused payment, but on legal advice paid in full prior to the Court Hearing.

Risk management lessons – the contractor protected their position well and the client's process was very slack in not picking up the qualified Bid.

---

7. <u>Unrealistic programs offered in the Bid</u>

Inaccurate and unrealistic development plans and construction programs create all sorts of repercussions for head contractors and their subcontractors, property developers, investment clients, lenders and insurers. I won't detail these repercussions here because they are largely self-evident, and are dealt with in detail in other sections of the book. There are several reasons why developers and contractors produce inaccurate and unrealistic programs, ranging from inexperience, excessive optimism or incompetence to more complex reasons which might have intended consequences, such as with the effect on cash flow.

It is such an important topic that I have devoted Chapter 21 entirely to it *(Planning and Programming)*.

8. <u>Undue interference on pricing and/or program</u> from internal or external sources, e.g. managers that love building legacy monuments; overbearing clients or shareholders.

People in authority interfere and over-ride risk management *'stop'* signs for a variety of reasons:

- Long-term clients lean on contractors to reduce their price *'if you want to keep our business'*, rationalising that this is guaranteed work for the contractor.
- Large shareholders think the stock price will be boosted if the company announces a lot of new business so they have a chat with their representatives on the Board, who have a chat with senior management.
- The company is having cash flow problems so senior management *'buy'* some projects to try and stay alive.
- Senior management and the directors think this particular project will be great for the company image and/or the stock price; don't worry too much if it is not profitable because the rest of the business is going well.

In these situations two things invariably happen:
▶ Middle management, who know the figures, are not informed of the real reasons and are left shaking their heads – and feeling insecure;
▶ Things don't work out for the best and the company incurs far greater losses than ever envisaged.

Sometimes, but not often, senior management do have some cards up their sleeve that will make the project profitable, but if so they should take the operational team into their confidence as soon as possible, e.g. with almost all projects the program has a direct bearing on profitability and if it can be substantially shortened for some reason then the project might be financially successful, but it also works the other way.

Risk management check points are put in Bid programs for prudent reasons, so ignore them and over-ride them at your peril. More than one small or medium building company has been brought down by just one or two projects.

9. <u>Bidding with annual revenue being the primary driver instead of profits</u>

Many companies, large and small, believe that the higher the turnover they generate each year the greater the chance of making a profit because of the financial gains they will make through creating improved efficiencies in delivery after winning projects, claims for variations and the squeezing of consultants and subcontractors during the life of the projects.

So with this in mind they cut margins, preliminaries and contingency allowances to the bone and chase turnover (revenue) as their primary objective, bidding and winning projects on little or no profit margin. They also justify this approach by convincing themselves that they will at least get some overheads for the head office even if the project only breaks even.

45

Now this may work sometimes but the construction industry is notorious for how many projects end up being unprofitable even when healthy allowances and margins are built into the winning price. So if you are chasing revenue and winning projects on an effective nil-margin basis then you are ultimately playing with fire. If anything goes wrong with time, cost and quality control then those slim margins or a break-even price will rapidly turn into a loss that will not be covered by variation claims and squeezing the subcontractors. And generally when this happens it is really bad news for the subcontractors.

On top of this the company balance sheet has to accommodate performance bonds, bank guarantees and retentions on the progress claims, so it is likely that the project cash flow will be negative overall if there is the slightest hiccup. If this situation occurs for a company with several projects concurrently then it will only be a matter of time until their bankers run out of patience.

Chasing revenue without profit is therefore a dangerous game for a construction company that does it often.

It is interesting to note how often construction companies make press releases announcing the new project they have won and its value. It would be of far greater interest to shareholders if they also announced their projected bottom line for that project as well, albeit with some cautionary qualifications. This is a good form of risk management in itself.

10. 'Super Profit' predictions over-riding established risk management procedures – two types of managers here – those that can only see 'blue sky', or those who are desperately trying to prop up the company when it is doing badly.

11. Inadequate cost escalation terms in contracts

    "Rise & Fall" is an intriguing contractual term and it is easy to think that "Fall" never happens, but it does occasionally and can cause some losses against budget. However it is far more likely that inflationary increases in labour and materials ("Rise") will be harmful and this can cause serious financial loss if not properly covered by the Terms of Contract. There are various formulae for this such as using a Consumer Price Index.

12. Inadequate currency change terms in contracts

    It is conventional wisdom that one of the quickest ways to go broke is to speculate on currency markets. With contracts involving cross-border currency transactions it is equally risky to have unhedged exposure, so it is not only prudent but also essential to safeguard against currency loss through hedging.

13. Failure to benchmark total bid value on a 'common sense' or 'logical' basis against comparable scope contracts.

    date stipulated in the contract. The reasons for such obstinate and frustrating behaviour can be many and varied and often as not it is cash flow driven, but not always.

How did this project 'escape' through all the risk management check points?

The project was a European motorway where the winning Bid was €400 m and the end cost was more than €600 m. The contract called for 38 kilometres of 4 lanes plus 2 emergency lanes through mountainous terrain, with 5.7 kilometres of tunnels (7 off), 5 large bridges from 130 to 400 metres in length, and a large amount of rock blasting out of the mountainside; 80 structures in all including entries and exits.

> Summary – on global comparison the €400m Bid price would have been competitive and probably tight for relatively easy terrain with no tunnelling, extensive rock blasting and large bridges. In hindsight, it is inexplicable how a quick and easy benchmarking like this did not stop the Bid consortium in their tracks. The end cost of more than €600m. did not contain any margin.
>
> Responsibility for the bidding and signing-off this project lay at several levels, from the estimators through to senior management, any of whom could have applied simple benchmarking. Is it possible that some more junior parties did highlight the problem but the *"grown-ups"* weren't for listening?

14. <u>Underestimating site and head office administrative costs and the time specifically required for the project, i.e. poor budgeting</u>

This is a common error, as people tend to be over-optimistic about the resources and time required to run a project, especially during the commissioning and completion period. Variations and Extensions of Time with daily costs can cover their own administrative costs but they will only partly alleviate basic miscalculations of program and resources for the overall project. There is no substitute for experience in this area of budgeting. PPPs in particular are often underestimated due to the demanding requirements for contractual delivery.

15. <u>Incorrect taxation assessments</u>

Tax is a field for the experts, but even they make mistakes when complex financial structures are involved, such as with PPPs. Tax liabilities and tax credits can both be miscalculated or overlooked and an independent second opinion is recommended as a prudent matter of course where large sums are involved.

With one large PPP investment a new finance director joined the concession company and 6 weeks after he arrived he advised the Board that he had found a $15m tax credit that could be claimed from 3 years previously. This had been missed by internal accounting, the external financial advisors and the auditors. Now that was worth an early bonus!

16. <u>*'Clever Clients'* who think they can do it better themselves by managing direct subcontractors</u> instead of wrapping the project into a lump sum contract with the primary risk being taken by the head contractor – a recipe for disaster.
http://en.wikipedia.org/wiki/The_Squaire

> **It is a problem when *"you don't know what you don't know"***

17. <u>Use of high risk new techniques or technologies</u> that have not had sufficient proving-out, causing big losses after winning the contract.

Projects are launched fairly regularly that have extremely high technical demands that are *"ground breaking"* and when successfully completed will also have a high profile. If the specifications for which the contractor has to guarantee performance delivery require new and unproven technology then all the danger signals should be flashing.

However the enthusiasm of senior management to win such projects and gain the high profile kudos on completion can sometimes overshadow and outweigh their pre-Bid investigations into how advanced and proven this new technology has been developed.

This is not always a simple situation and depends heavily on the technical people being entirely open and frank about the status of the technological development, because it is likely that the contractor's senior management will not have an in-depth understanding of the new technology. The technical people might be over-optimistic because this is their *"big opportunity"*, or they may have only proven the technology in laboratory testing and be taking a leap of faith that it will work in a commercial situation.

The obvious answer is that the risks are carried by those directly responsible for the technical delivery and performance and the contracts and subcontracts should be drawn up carefully to reflect this, with appropriate guarantees and indemnities.

Clients will take the view that *"if you promise to deliver the contract and you do, you will get paid, but if you don't deliver then it is going to cost you"*.

There is a wide range of industries in which this situation can apply in today's world of fast moving technical development, from prison security systems to "clean room" chip manufacturing factories.

Two highly expensive and publicly known examples in recent years have been:

The National Physics Laboratory, UK
http://www.nao.org.uk/publications/0506/the_termination_of_the_pfi_con.aspx

and

Siemens Particle Therapy Oncology Hospital, Kiel, Germany

http://www.marketwatch.com/story/siemens-ends-particle-therapy-project-in-kiel-2011-09-14

http://www.siemens.com/press/en/pressrelease/?press=/en/pressrelease/2011/corporate_communication/axx20110983.htm

Sometimes client specifications and expectations are unrealistic and sometimes suppliers and contractors offer more than they prudently should.

18. Conversely, the failure of project management or technical people to *'move with the times'* and use more efficient technical or management procedures that have been proven – you can lose bids because of this.

19. Poor communications and relationship management with client, government authorities, subcontractors and suppliers. Get off on the wrong foot and it is hard to recover. **Listen hard to what the client is saying** – it can win you the project. Same with the community and media after winning the project.

20. Political risk – this can be difficult to assess, but many major contractors have incurred heavy losses when governments pull the rug towards the close of bidding after a great deal of time and cost has been expended by the Bidders. This is a real breach of good faith. Bidders know that only one of them will win and that is fair competition, but they certainly do not appreciate being strung along. It helps if the particular government agency agrees to pay compensation as in the following situation http://www.adelaidenow.com.au/news/south-australia/compensation-for-cancelled-prison-bidders/story

Design, Construction, Commissioning and Transition to Operations

21. Failure to line up a competent project team sufficiently ahead of the project award, especially the project director (this applies equally to D&C and PPP teams).

22. Lack of continuity of personnel from Bid to D&C – and through to operations if it is a PPP. When this happens it is all too easy to blame others for problems arising.

23. Hiring inexperienced and under-qualified management resources is a serious trap and false economy.

24. Too many contract managers hired in, because many have no real company allegiance or loyalty and it is just another job. Even worse, if they get a better offer mid-way through the project they are likely to leave at short notice.

25. Project directors and construction managers in key positions must be good communicators Poor communicators cause all sorts of problems. There are several references to this throughout this book.

26. Denial, stubbornness and bloody-mindedness by headstrong *'sledge hammer'* construction managers can be really damaging if they do not identify and report potential risks at the earliest possible time, but keep the problem to themselves in the belief that they can fix it before it gets worse or before anyone above finds out. Managers with this sort of attitude cause real relationship damage in any event and should not be tolerated.

The construction industry unfortunately has an inherent culture of breeding a proportion of dominating 'sledge hammer' site managers who are nearly always bad communicators as well and yell and scream at everyone. These types of managers invariably end up with poor relationships with clients and subcontractors, more than a reasonable number of disputes, poor team spirit and a lack of respect from their own staff.

Compare this to real leaders who communicate well with everyone; mentor and motivate; have all the skills to show the way; command respect from all stakeholders; and do not need to raise their voice

27. Slow start (particularly if the program is tight anyway)

28. Fast start – fast-tracking with inadequate preparation, resulting in unbudgeted costs and most probably costly rework. (See Chapter 21 on S-Curves)

29. Basic changes to design after commencement – this is costly for both the client and the contractor; the client has to pay for the design changes and may well have a delayed completion and commencement of revenue; and the contractor because of the delays incurred, the true costs of which are rarely fully recouped.

30. Failing to accurately track and document design and equipment changes and getting them signed off; and also failing to raise timely cost variations.

31. Insufficient independent in-house or external overview (see Chapters 27 and 28)

32. Poor subcontract management and payment – can cause serious construction delay (see item 35 below).

33. Undercapitalised subcontractors who cannot survive slow cash flow or a significant loss on a particular project.

34. Head contractors that have inadequate financial capacity – contractors need to have sufficient working capital for the size and complexity of the project. Major investors and governments can get caught out by contracting with Tier 2 contractors who might initially appear to have the financial capacity but then find that the size and complexity is greater than they can manage and finance.

35. Clients and head contractors that are chronically bad payers.

It is not uncommon to come across clients that simply refuse on principle and without any proper contractual justification to make full and timely payments even though the progress and variation claims have been independently certified for payment. This type of client likes to find spurious reasons to only pay say 85% of each certificate and then mostly later than the date stipulated in the contract. The reasons for such obstinate and frustrating behaviour can be many and varied and often as not it is cash flow driven, but not always.

Some head contractors do the same with their subcontractors, but they overlook the fact that subcontractors and suppliers generally respond in direct proportion to the way they are treated and if it is really unreasonable then the bad payer will pay more in the long run, one way or another. This sort of practice can be really damaging to relationships, but conversely if payments are made promptly then the subcontractors will often go the extra mile for their client and work harder to meet the program and possibly not bother to claim for some unexpected costs they have encountered. It is a two way street and it takes only a small amount of goodwill to generate significant performance improvements.

Contractors do not have a problem with claims that are challenged for valid reasons provided there is an open and honest debate about the situation, but clients that short-change and are late with every payment as a matter of course are infuriating and are of course in breach of good faith as well as breach of contract.

Of course contractors are not angels either and often put in grossly inflated claims or claims for work that is not completed or where the milestone has not been reached.

Project Leadership – How Bad Can It Get?

▶ **Lessons to learn from grossly incompetent site management**

Note: for legal reasons the identity of the following project cannot be disclosed, but the facts described are an accurate description of events.

The following story describes a project that ran off the rails well and truly and how it was brought back on track. It all went wrong because the project director was completely out of his depth and also had the wrong personal skills to be leading the project. It demonstrates the need for robust risk management processes at all stages in a contract to protect the client; the contractor; subcontractors and suppliers. **This factual account shows how project leadership is vital to success.**

This was an industrial D&C with a contract value of $140m and a 3 1/2 year program. Not a large project in itself but a vitally important one because it was a critical component in a much larger complex, with the rest of the industrial complex having activities that fed off this facility. The Scope of Works was very detailed in respect of the deliverables and the Contract was tight, especially in regard to the program, with heavy liquidated damages to a cap of 40% of the contract value, recoverable over 5 months of delay subject to other extenuating circumstances.

The Contractor was a subsidiary of an international company who were recognised leaders in this field. They had no other involvement with the rest of the industrial complex, but were engaged because of the criticality of this particular facility. The Contractor hired an outside construction director rather than appointing someone from inside the company and they commenced on site with a suitably experienced team of 14 personnel.

Three months before the due completion date the client raised urgent concerns about the progress whereupon the Contractor advised they would be 4 months late and subsequently produced an updated program. Two months before the new completion date the client concluded that this date was clearly not possible. The Contractor then advised that they would require another 7 months, i.e. completion would be 11 months later than the original Contract completion date.

The client demanded urgent expediting action, so the parent company of the Contractor appointed an external audit team to review the entire project and make recommendations. For the parent company, this contract value was actually quite small in the context of their annual global revenue, so they had not been keeping a close eye on the project. For the client, the Liquidated Damages that would likely apply were far less important than the serious flow-on effect to the overall industrial complex.

The client demanded urgent expediting action, so the parent company of the Contractor appointed an external audit team to review the entire project and make recommendations. For the parent company, this contract value was actually quite small in the context of their annual global revenue, so they had not been keeping a close eye on the project. For the client, the Liquidated Damages that would likely apply were far less important than the serious flow-on effect to the overall industrial complex.

The independent audit team appointed consisted of a project manager, quantity surveyor and planner. Whilst all were very experienced and had been involved in many difficult projects internationally, they were taken aback by the problems on this particular project.

- They were introduced to the construction director by the national Managing Director, but immediately after he left the site the construction director said he would throw them off the site if they did anything without his approval. After a swift tour of the site he then declined any sort of cooperation – no programs; no subcontractor information; no access to interview team members on site. So, the Managing Director was quickly recalled by the audit team!

- Behaviour only marginally improved. Senior members of the site team were threatened with dismissal if they talked to the audit team, so the Managing Director was recalled again!

- The audit team spent 4 days reviewing the status of the works; the subcontractor arrangements; cost reports and interviewing the key site management personnel; following which they produced their initial findings and recommendations, including:

- The master program dated 5 months earlier had not been revised since and was showing a number of activities as completed that had not even started. The full-time planner/programmer said he was only allowed to produce what the construction director instructed - and he was not allowed to check progress on site. The construction director had for some time been seriously misleading the client and his own head office about the progress by delivering false programs.

- There was a similar situation with the project accounts, which showed many dubious counter-claims against subcontractors as being fact and, with these assumptions, indicated that the total project costs were within the original budget. This was clearly misleading and the end result was a 50% cost over-run, not including substantial Liquidated Damages.

- There were 22 specialist subcontractors and properly resourced there should have been 700 workers on site, but 18 of the subcontractors had no personnel on site and the remaining 4 had about 30 between them.

- All of the subcontractors were in dispute with the Contractor for a wide variety of reasons, including unreasonable back-charges. The construction director had stopped payment of all claims in an attempt to force the subcontractors to concede on the disputes, with these stopped payments including a substantial number of standard progress payments certified by the Engineer.

- The Anticipated Final Cost Report failed to reflect the extent of costs and liabilities to complete the works.

- All but 4 members of the site team were working on the disputed claims and back-charges on the instructions of the construction director; in many cases spending a lot of time trying to build a case when there wasn't one.

- The four site managers who were actively trying to keep the site going were capable people, but they were all on the point of walking out through sheer frustration.

- Several of the activities that had not been started could not start because they required planning approval, with some needing a 3 to 4 months lead time, and the applications had not even been prepared, let alone submitted.

The construction director was obsessed with "squashing" subcontractors. He had completely lost sight of delivering the project. He admitted in interview that he had only read the Scope of Works and had not read the Contract thoroughly at any time in the past 3 years and he stated that it was unimportant because he knew what was required technically. Clearly he had no idea of the obligations under the Contract and did not seem to comprehend the significance to the overall complex.

It turned out that whilst the construction director was an experienced and capable design engineer he had never actually undertaken project management and had no idea about efficient methods and processes.

He camouflaged his lack of experience by heavily bullying his team, the suppliers and subcontractors and would not tolerate any other opinions, constructive or dissenting. His arrogance and rudeness had to be seen to be believed.

He was relieved of his duties a few days after the initial report from the audit team and replaced by a properly experienced construction manager.

The independent audit team rapidly made several other expediting recommendations, with the priorities being:

- Restoration of the subcontractors' cash flow and freezing of the disputed claims and back-charges, pending a realistic review of them. The restored trust of the subcontractors took high importance.

- Urgent attention to planning applications and approvals.

- Acceleration works by all the subcontractors on a 24/7 basis (the cost was actually far less than the potential damages).

- Creating realistic and accurate programs that were effective as management tools, both the master program and separate component programs.

- The project achieved commissioning and practical completion four months after the audit team was engaged to the extent of effective integration with the larger complex, although some minor less important works still took a few more months to close out. Needless to say, the Contractor suffered heavy financial losses and some loss of reputation, although the latter was somewhat recovered through taking the drastic actions required to recover the situation.

LESSONS LEARNED

- The leadership skills of the construction director are paramount and must cover knowledge of the contract, technical and programming competence, methods and processes, as well as the important personal skills of communications and relationship management that engender motivation and team spirit.

- If efficient risk management processes had been in place the alarm bells would have started ringing a year or more earlier and the parent company would have had the opportunity to rectify the situation and instigate changes to enable completion on time and to mitigate the potential losses.

- A project may seem small in the overall context for an international company, but even 'small' projects have the potential to cause heavy financial and reputational loss.

- The client's project monitoring had also been quite slack, although they did identify the problem and demand action from the Contractor's parent company. Clients can protect themselves inexpensively by engaging independent project auditors to monitor on their behalf.

An Overview of Changes in the Construction Industry since the 'Eighties

By John Messenger MSc BSc CEng FICE FIStructE MAPM
Director Driver Trett Group

As we sit here in 2014 looking back on the developments in the construction industry over the last 30 years it may seem that very little has changed in terms of the way in which we build things. The
By John Messenger MSc BSc CEng FICE FIStructE MAPM
Director Driver Trett Group

As we sit here in 2014 looking back on the developments in the construction industry over the last 30 years it may seem that very little has changed in terms of the way in which we build things. The construction methods used on sites still bear a striking similarity to that which would have been seen in the 1980's and before, although we do recognise that there have been developments in materials technology, design techniques, health and safety and the protection of the environment.

There have however been profound changes to the industry in the way in which it is structured and carries on its business. Despite these changes, some which are explored in more detail below, there does not appear to have been any reduction in the potential for things to go wrong and projects still overrun on cost and time on a sadly regular basis.

Influences for structural change

Throughout the 1970's, 80's and 90's there were a number of influences for change in the construction industry including:

- Demands for greater efficiency (Latham (1994) & Egan (1998) reports in the UK)
- The need for less fragmentation between consultants and construction specialists
- Client pressure to pass more risk to the contractor
- Acceptance of the need for increased health and safety and general procedural protection
- Increased focus on corporate governance and competition

Changes in the structure of the industry

From a time when the majority of construction was undertaken on a traditional 'client/consultant designed' and 'contractor built' formula, we have moved to a situation in which clients seek better value for money and to move the risks associated with construction from themselves to the contractor. Contractors accept greater competition and many also accept the transfer of risks which they see as a means of distinguishing themselves in the race to win more work and in the belief that this creates room for enhanced profits. This change has created a significant shift in the way in which the industry operates as Contractors have developed significant in-house design capability and consultants have polarised between larger organisations (some of which have developed facilities management and other quasi-contractor services) and a large number of small specialist organisations. As this is being written it is clear that even greater consolidation is now taking place as the major players combine and structure themselves to be able to take on the ever increasing scale of the major projects worldwide.

Changes in the way in which the industry operates have also caused a shift towards freelance employment and the use of employment/staff agencies to supply people for single project engagements. The perception of construction as an employment choice in a quickly advancing technological world and changes in employment law have perhaps also had an influence on the industry and the ways in which it copes with the ups and downs of project related work. Computer and communications technology now allow work to be done quicker and with fewer people and has reinforced pressures driving the move to narrower specialisation. In recent times the effect of the changes has been clearly seen in the shortage of qualified and competent staff resources available to man jobs anywhere in the world.

Changes in the way in which construction (infrastructure in its widest sense) is procured

Perhaps the biggest shift however has been the move to outsourcing the provision of infrastructure as governments recognise the ever increasing demand for infrastructure and the need to move this burden from government spending to the private sector. Under the influence of this pressure the industry has moved significantly towards being part of an infrastructure service sector rather than just a construction business.

PPP and the other various BOOT, BOT etc. forms of procurement in particular, represent a fundamentally different procurement approach to infrastructure from that which both the client and contractors have traditionally been used to. Traditionally clients have engaged consultants to design projects and have then engaged contractors to build them. The lines of responsibility, the method of payment and the risks involved were understood by both sides.

PPP procurement requires contractors to develop their offerings from simple construction to full service provision offerings, frequently within a concession type arrangement. To do this, they have to form relationships with a number of other organisations in order to provide the full scope of the project (finance, design, construct, operate and maintain) and to accept a much wider set of risks including business, revenue and full construction risk. PPP arrangements have moved away from traditional construction and cover much longer contract periods and focus on services and not on built infrastructure.

The following extract from Wikipedia (April 2014) describes the introduction of PPPs

"Pressure to change the standard model of public procurement arose initially from concerns about the level of public debt, which grew rapidly during the macroeconomic dislocation of the 1970s and 1980s. Governments sought to encourage private investment in infrastructure, initially on the basis of accounting fallacies arising from the fact that public accounts did not distinguish between recurrent and capital expenditures.

The idea that private provision of infrastructure represented a way of providing infrastructure at no cost to the public has now been generally abandoned; however, interest in alternatives to the standard model of public procurement persisted. In particular, it has been argued that models involving an enhanced role for the private sector, with a single private-sector organization taking responsibility for most aspects of service provisions for a given project, could yield an improved allocation of risk, while maintaining public accountability for essential aspects of service provision.

Initially, most public–private partnerships were negotiated individually, as one-off deals, and much of this activity began in the early 1990s.

In 1992, the UK government introduced the private finance initiative (PFI), the first systematic program aimed at encouraging public–private partnerships."

Economic considerations are not, of course, limited to the UK and the introduction of PPP procurement has changed the face of construction in countries that have moved their economies towards privately financed infrastructure. Many larger contractors have seen the advantage of the longer term concession contracts as a means of providing business stability and have converted themselves into facilities management and concession companies in which construction has moved towards being a subsidiary activity and which some have even dropped altogether. At the same time financial institutions have recognised the advantages of infrastructure as an asset class and have moved to take up an increasing proportion of the funding requirement.

The development of the PPP market has not been quick or without its difficulties and has passed through a number of transitional stages during which both sides of the procurement divide have developed and learnt from their mistakes. Both sides have regularly failed to appreciate the changed relationship and have permitted hidden agendas of those opposed to outsourced infrastructure (and development in general) to cloud and delay projects. In particular the change has been resisted as:

- Traditional contractors have seen a risk to their position as simple constructors and have resisted the impact of wider scope of work and the inevitable JV arrangements as they try and retain their traditional contract risk profile with access to claims for technical and program risks.
- Government employees and their unions have resisted an opening up of government activities to the private sector.
- Clients have sought to retain the ability to define the design and to avoid exposure to the kinds of solutions that the market might otherwise deliver.
- Government procurement procedure has remained focused on a hands-off engagement with bidders which has set up a non-collaborative, contract driven, risk dumping, 'lose-lose' relationship instead of a partnership driven 'win-win' situation.

These ingrained attitudes have served to pervert the process and have left the whole PPP procurement system at risk of criticism by its various detractors. Even projects which have been heralded as a success have often focused on the legitimisation of unnecessary excess rather than the sensible delivery of function at appropriate levels of specification and cost.

Notwithstanding this the spread of PPPs within the leading countries (Canada, Australia, USA, UK and much of Europe) has been appreciable with project numbers running into the thousands as both businesses and governments have welcomed the change.

The polarised judgements of the two sides of the debate on the relative merits of the experience to date are unlikely to be reliable and the volume of bad press might have been enough by now to have discredited and consigned the whole PPP arena to history if it were not for the simple underlying fact that **governments cannot afford to meet national infrastructure requirements without private sector involvement.** Discussion of the relative merits of money being raised by private versus public means and whether PPPs represent privatisation by the back door are largely irrelevant, as it is frequently a simple decision between to have a project or not.

For PPPs to be a real success in the future these hidden agendas and attitudes will need to be removed from both sides and both sides will need to address their respective responsibilities to engage in delivering appropriate value and the nature of the long term partnership.

The further development of sophisticated concession based procurement of any governmental service side activity that is capable of being transferred to the private sector represents a major objective if governments are to keep public spending (and corresponding tax levels) to a minimum and to focus their efforts on the core business of government.

Where do we go from here?

Over the same timespan there has been a proliferation of contract forms aimed at providing a standard form to cover every eventuality, such as the FIDIC Rainbow Suite and the NEC Suite of Contracts and variations of these as produced in many countries as local standard forms.

Whilst this attention to new forms of contract and the balancing of risk between the parties is welcome it is not clear that it has improved the situation appreciably in reducing the level of disputes that arise.

The benefits that might have accrued from better contracts seem to have been offset by a reduction in the ability of organisations to manage their people to effectively deliver the projects.

Central to most disputes remains the lack of any rigour in the management of the construction program. Amazing as it is, many contractors do not program the works in detail (perhaps preferring not to have an accurate record) and many clients do not specify a definitive program regime. Contracts typically assign responsibility for programming but fail to provide a means of dealing with the problem of non-compliance. This alone leaves these contracts unmanageable and the resolution of disputes as a 'global claim' farce. Within the melee that surrounds most projects, client organisations appear to prefer the cover that arbitration and other legal processes give them whilst contractors, faced with extended cash-flow problems, play the expanded claims value game as a means of maximising their belated returns. The consequence is that disputes have grown in size and the time taken to deal with them has lengthened.

Some industry sectors have developed a more realistic approach to major construction investment projects (typically the oil, gas and process industries). The major feature of these projects which differs from normal infrastructure situations is the understanding of the project as an investment and the need by the client to deliver that investment (as part of a much larger overall business) as rapidly and cost effectively as possible. In such circumstances the balancing of risk is more realistic as clients recognise the need to take the main responsibility and to cover off their construction partners against risks that they have no real ability or interest in taking.

This same common sense approach does not usually apply within other infrastructure client bodies (often government bodies), who see lowest possible cost and complete de-risking of the public sector position as attractive positions.

Some major construction client bodies have however sought to establish their own specific arrangements with the industry by developing sophisticated bespoke management systems. Some have made valiant attempts to incorporate many of the relationship and softer issues that inevitably are at the centre of all contract performance. Has this made a difference? It is not clear to an outsider that the efforts on major projects have led to more economical project delivery however it is likely to have met with some success in terms of dependability of the end date. Projects that receive such attention are however few in number and similar efforts are probably not going to be replicated in the smaller (but still sizeable) jobs, let alone major infrastructure projects in developing nations (the bulk of the infrastructure market).

Commitment to risk management and the timely/prompt settlement of problems

Better control of human and political behaviour is undoubtedly now central to our industry. A better understanding of human dynamics and its impact on the management of the risks is essential if major failures are to be avoided. A change of emphasis is required which encourages clients and contractors to join together to deliver their projects. To do this clients and contractors will both have to bring greater professionalism and rigour to their work and perhaps go back to a time when preparation work was done comprehensively.

Much of this book focusses on examples of PPPs however the principles are applicable to many present-day 'design and build' procurement formats in which the responsibility for risk is largely transferred from the client to the contractor. The duration of these contracts can be much longer than the simple construction contracts of the past, the scope of work is more complex and the potential areas of dispute are much larger. A collaborative partnership arrangement is needed with significantly better client/contractor/service provider relationship management under which risks, disputes and any other contentious issues are dealt with continuously and are never postponed.

Conclusion

The changes in the construction industry have been positive in many areas and have seen a shift from a simple construction focus to one of infrastructure provision. Infrastructure is a major worldwide requirement and looks likely to remain so for more than the foreseeable future. Delivery performance, service provision and relationship management are going to become the key factors in determining long term success or failure.

If this book helps to recognise the importance of human dynamics on projects and encourages a more realistic attitude towards adopting sensible and practical risk management procedures then it will serve the industry well in the future.

Biography – John Messenger

John is a Director within the Driver Group (an international consultancy offering commercial, contractual, procurement and management services to the construction industry) where he is responsible for Project Management and the Groups' PPP services. John has over 35 years of international experience in the construction industry in both contracting and consultancy and so is aware of both sides of the business; his experience includes the management of projects through initial feasibility studies, scheme development, and the financial structuring necessary to translate an opportunity into a viable and deliverable business enterprise.

John has direct practical experience of the identification of procurement strategies and of defining the procurement processes necessary to secure the involvement of project partners on realistic commercial and contractual terms. He has direct practical experience of working for owners seeking to develop projects, as well as for contractors during project tendering, negotiation and delivery stages.

Factors which have Influenced Change in the UK Construction Industry — A Client's Perspective

By Ian Williams MSc, DIC, CEng, FICE, FCIArb
Former Head of Projects for the Government Olympic Executive, London 2012
Executive Manager for the Supreme Committee for the Qatar 2022 World Cup

(An extract from a keynote speech given at the Czech Tunnelling Association One Day Seminar, Prague, 2010)

I have had the privilege of working on a number of large projects in the UK and overseas from the late 1980s to present day, spanning the watershed of the period of unsuccessful and successful projects in the UK.

This paper looks at the events and changes which the author considers contributed to the change in attitude and behaviour which underpinned the successes of civil engineering and tunnelling projects in the UK from the late 1990s onwards. The paper also puts forward what the author sees as the key elements that make up a framework for a successful project outcome.

There have been six broad factors or changes that have been influential in getting the UK construction industry to the position it is in today, these being:

- UK society and economic pressure - a desire for change
- Contract and procurement changes
- Catastrophic events i.e. Heathrow collapse 1994
- Legislative changes related to Health and Safety
- Insurance industry pressure
- Clients insistence on achieving planned outcomes

UK society and economic pressure - desire for change

In 1994, in the wake of several poorly performing projects, the UK government commissioned a report, the Latham Report. Its objective was to review procurement and contractual arrangements in the UK construction industry with the aim of improving the quality and efficiency of UK construction. The report condemned the existing industry practices as: 'ineffective', 'adversarial', 'fragmented', 'incapable of delivering for its customers', and 'lacking respect for its employees'. The report made 53 recommendations with an underlying message of urging the industry to reform and advocate partnering and collaboration by construction companies.

This report was followed up by the Egan Report 1998 which was commissioned again by the UK government. The scope of this was to look at construction from a Clients' perspective and supplement the Latham Report to accelerate change and to make the industry more responsive to the needs of its customers. Five key drivers for change were identified: committed leadership, a focus on the customer, integrated processes and teams, a quality driven agenda and commitment to people.

Contract and procurement changes

Towards the end of the 1980s some clients mostly in the water related industry had adopted the use of the Institution of Chemical Engineers form of contract, (known commonly as the 'Green Book'). This contract was considered a less adversarial contract based on a form of cost reimbursement. Despite the use of the 'Green Book' there was still a strong view that there was a need for a contract with simpler language, clearer allocation of responsibilities and fundamentally less adversarial than was commonly being used by the wider construction industry (this being the Institution of Civil Engineers (ICE) Condition of Contract). In 1993, the first edition of the New Engineering Contract (NEC) form of contract was launched. Not surprisingly, The Latham Report in 1994 recommended and endorsed the use of NEC. In July 2010 the ICE announced that it would solely endorse the NEC3 suite of contracts and withdraw ICE Conditions of Contract first published in 1945. This was a huge watershed in the evolution of the NEC and the mood within the industry.

Furthermore, clients such as BAA developed their own form of contract for major construction works. BAA developed the T5 Agreement (the Contract) for the Terminal 5 development. The T5 Agreement was a unique contract because the Agreement outlined processes and strategies to manage successful project outcomes in an uncertain environment. It did not outline contractual positions when things go wrong but **focused on principles such as behaviours and relationships, people, risk management, performance, success and people as individuals contributing to integrated teams to achieve a common goal.** The three fundamental working principles considered essential to make the Agreement work were Trust, Commitment and Teamwork.

Catastrophic events i.e. Heathrow tunnel collapse, 1994

On the 21st October 1994 a major collapse associated with NATM works occurred on the Heathrow Express project. Fortunately nobody was killed but the incident eventually resulted in prosecutions. More importantly, the event was a catalyst for change in behaviour, attitude and approach within the UK construction industry.

Legislative changes – Health & Safety management

In 1995, the Construction (Design and Management) Regulations came into force. These regulations represented a major change in how the construction industry managed Health & Safety. For the first time the duties of clients and designers were made explicit. It also reflected a change from complex and bureaucratic regulations to more focus on risk and influencing the attitudes and behaviour of duty holders. These regulations were revised in 1997 and 2002 to take on feedback from industry wide consultation.

Insurance industry pressure

In October 2001, the Association of British Insurers (ABI), representing insurers and re-insurers on the London–based Insurance Market, contacted the British Tunnelling Society (BTS) to voice their growing concerns about recent losses associated with tunnelling works both in the UK and overseas. The ABI sought to work with 'industry' to develop a 'Joint Code of Practice' for better management of the risks associated with tunnelling works and in 2003 the 'The Joint Code of Practice for Risk Management of Tunnel Works in the UK' was launched, with the objective of promoting and securing best practice for the minimisation and management of risks associated with the design and construction of 'Tunnel Works'.

Clients' insistence on achieving planned outcomes

The 1990s saw a change from projects sponsored by the public sector to those promoted by the private sector. Much of this shift was due to privatisation of infrastructure companies with the discipline of accountability to shareholders and the need for planned certainties. The result of this was knowledgeable clients demanding planned outcomes to deliver successful major infrastructures safely, on time and within budget.

Conclusion - a Framework for Successful Outcomes

From my experience, there are five key framework components for delivering successful outcomes. These factors are inter-related and provide a platform for the next element or stage of the project to build on.

Competence – This starts with the Client. The Client must be competent in leadership, planning, technical issues, have the right behavioural and people skills and be prepared to accept and manage risk. Much of the same skills are needed by the Constructor and Designer.

The Right Contract – A non-adversarial form of contract provides an environment that competent people can use as a platform that encourages the resolution of issues and fair commercial outcomes. This allows engineers to get on with solving problems and engineering rather than spending a great proportion of their time protecting company commercial positions.

Right Behaviours – It's not enough to have competent people and the right contract, those people must have the right behavioural skills to make it happen. This can be summarised as people who are committed to three basic working principles based on behaviour, these being: Trust, Commitment and Teamwork.

Commitment to Risk Management – This is central to understanding the challenges and how best to manage them. This should be central to the management's approach of the project and all key team members should be committed to managing the process.

Processes – appropriate processes are needed which provide the 'checks and balance' required to manage the risks identified. These range from planning, the design process and costing, through to the construction process.

Biography – Ian Williams

Ian is a Chartered Engineer and a Fellow of the Institution of Civil Engineers and Institute of Arbitrators. He has 25 years' experience in major engineering projects in the UK, Southern Africa, the Middle East and South East Asia. Ian is currently responsible for infrastructure and transport aspects for the Qatar 2022 World Cup for the Supreme Committee. Before joining the Supreme Committee, he was Head of Projects for the Government Olympic Executive on the London 2012 Olympic Games. Prior to the Olympics, he held key positions on the delivery of metros in London and Singapore, and airport infrastructure developments at Heathrow for Terminal 5 and the redevelopment of Terminals 3 & 4.

Public Private Partnerships
– full of potential risks

PPPs now form a significant part of the investment and construction landscape in dozens of countries and whereas the pipeline for them has decreased in some regions such as Western Europe it is very strong and growing in many other regions. PPPs are all about 'risk transfer' and as such warrant considerable discussion in any debate about risk management.

The Pros and Cons of the Concept and the implications of having such a complex suite of contracts

PPP projects are contractually quite complex compared to other forms of design and construction contracting. In the early days of PPPs, in the '90s and early 2000s, this contractual complexity left the field open to a lot of misunderstanding and a lack of alignment between the various stakeholders and it was a minefield for disputes, because of the ambiguities and grey areas in the suite of contracts, even gaping black holes.

Human dynamics take on many forms in this climate. Today the contract documents have been refined and the majority of participants in developed countries at least have a good understanding of how PPPs work; and experience is being rapidly gained in developing nations.
Nevertheless, human behaviours are still one of the most important dynamics in PPPs because they are partnerships between the public and private sector. Whilst these parties have many objectives in common, they do at the same time have conflicting interests and this scenario can require skilful and sensitive handling by managers from both sides of the fence.

Before exploring the human dynamics that arise in PPPs, we provide the following brief overview of the PPP concept so that readers can understand the bigger picture and in turn why the human factors and behaviours arise.

PPPs normally consist of four primary contracts; the Project Agreement, Finance Agreement, D&C Contract and FM Services Contract. Alongside these are numerous other contractual and supporting documents, such as the original Bid brief, scope of works, the design and equipment drawings and specifications, collateral warranties, etc.

The major benefit of PPPs is the transfer of risk from the public to the private sector in respect of:

- Total capital costs
- The delivery program
- Operations and maintenance delivery and costs
- Life cycle replacement
- Quality and standards of services and equipment
- Revenues in capacity contracts, e.g. road tolls

Critics of PPPs, most of whom appear be ideologically based, conveniently forget that the history of government procurement worldwide has for decades been one of 20% to 50% (or greater) cost and program overruns. This has been typical in both developed and developing countries.

Additional to this, O&M and lifecycle replacement budgets have traditionally been quite inadequate, resulting in progressively run-down facilities and standards of the facilities, e.g. schools and hospitals in most countries.

In further response to PPP critics, any (supposed) increased cost of funding, which is generally their biggest beef, is virtually insignificant compared to the aforementioned cost overruns that occur under normal government procurement.

PPP financing generally consists of equity ranging from 10% (social projects) to 30% (roads) and the balance in debt. The cost of the debt is normally line-ball or only slightly higher than the rates that governments can obtain. Therefore the additional cost of the funding relates to the return required by the Concessionaire for their long term investment, mostly 20 to 30 years. As a rule of thumb, competition restricts this to an IRR range of 11% to 13%. This is not a high return for taking on the above risks for the term of the concession.

So, to show this in practical terms, take a $100m social project, say a hospital, with a 10% equity ratio and 90% debt at an interest cost of say 6% pa. Allow the Concessionaire an additional 6% return on his equity, 12% in total, in return for taking all the contractual risk. This extra 6% on the $10m equity amounts to $600,000 per year on a reducing basis as the equity is amortised over the period of the concession; or looking at it another way this is 0.6% p.a. on the total $100m.

History has proven time and again that this is chicken feed compared to the alternative costs of normal government procurement, let alone taking into account the on-going poor maintenance and life cycle replacement. The same critics might say that the $100m capital cost is inflated by the O&M and life cycle costs built into the financial model. This is not a valid criticism, because these allocations are spent over time and this is reflected in the financial model.

There are different ways of structuring PPP funding. Mostly it is the straightforward debt and equity model, but in Canada there are several projects in which the State partner has injected a substantial sum as a subsidy, in some cases 50% or more of the total capital cost over the life of the concession as determined in the financial model. The Concessionaire still adopts most of the operational risk and the risk of return on their equity, but with the State having substantial "skin in the Game" the two parties really are in a partnership that engenders close cooperation.

The same critics, as previously mentioned, often complain about the fact that PPP funding is off the government balance sheets and that this is a dangerous scenario long-term. Some Governments are very aware of this and allocate the entire PPP funding cost to their annual budget in the year of financial close, e.g. the Victorian State Government in Australia, which is very experienced in PPP structuring and management.

To give a balanced overview, there is one aspect of the PPP process that in the view of most Concessionaires is very much a negative, this being the high level of Bid costs.

They are generally considered to be ridiculously out of proportion to the potential for return and the percentage probability of winning a PPP project. Furthermore the margins on a PPP are too slim for a Concessionaire to be able to recover lost Bid costs from the last Bid on the next one, if successful.

This has led to many smaller investors (potential Concessionaires) pulling out of the market. The big investors in the PPP market have been forced to take straight write-offs and for most it took many years to obtain a portfolio of PPP investments that is big enough to comfortably absorb an annual allocation for lost bid costs. Even so the big operators are not happy with the current process.

So, there has to be a better way. One way would be for the government client to manage and firm up the initial design and then put the project out to competitive bidding. Currently we have the ridiculous situation in most countries whereby in a typical project three or more bidders will each spend a fortune on preparing a full design to probably 1:200 scale, only to see all but one of these designs thrown into the rubbish bin at the end of the day.

Governments argue that if they handle the design process then they will not get the benefit of innovation that comes out of a competitive situation. Many people disagree with this view and believe it is something that can be managed effectively.

An extreme example of a huge waste of bidding costs was the Brisbane Airport Link project in Australia in 2009, in which 3 consortia supposedly each spent around $20m on their respective Bids, with only one winner of course, so $40m of valuable company working capital (shareholders' funds) went down the drain. The largest percentage of this expenditure was for civil engineering design, yet realistically there are only a small number of different ways that you can design motorways, tunnels and bridges.

Is it really essential to see which Bidder can come up with something really different by way of innovation, especially in a motorway? Ultimately, this will drive even the big players from the market.

There have been some changing trends in approach to PPPs recently and one of significance is that investors (Concessionaires) are no longer prepared to take traffic volume and toll risk. There have been a series of toll roads that have been financial failures due to lack of traffic. In each case the tolls were calculated on the basis of traffic projections by expert consultants and by the local traffic authority, with these projections then being calculated into a toll that would support the financial requirements. However, it has been found by hard experience that there is a widespread public non-acceptance of tolls unless they are quite low and PPP tolls generally have not met this test.

The alternative approach, which is now being widely used globally, is the "availability" model whereby the State pays the Concessionaire an annual amount that covers the cost and amortisation of debt and equity and the costs of operations and maintenance, all out of user-funded taxes in the same manner as a non-PPP. There is a deduction regime if the unavailability of the motorway exceeds the agreed programmed maintenance closures.

The following toll roads in Australia had significantly lower than expected traffic volumes and toll revenues, causing serious financial difficulties:

- Cross City Tunnel, Sydney
- Lane Cove Tunnel, Sydney
- Clem Jones Tunnel & Motorway, Brisbane
- Airport Link, Brisbane

In Germany the Herren Tunnel at Lübeck has also had significantly lower than anticipated traffic volumes. These experiences and other similar ones have been instrumental in the switch to the "availability" model around the world.

On a final note, one of the real benefits of PPPs is the partnering aspect and community participation. If a PPP is to be successful, as the great majority are, then all stakeholders must genuinely embrace the community aspects of being respectful partners and adhering to open, honest and constant communications. This has meant a sea-change in attitude for many stakeholders and building companies in particular.

Tips to keep out of trouble

Structuring, Bidding and Finalising the Financing and the Contract

- Vital to understand the risk transfer differences between traditional D&C and PPPs – make sure there are no gaps between the contracts.
- Services abatement risk transfer terms – beware of caps in the Service Provider's (FM) Subcontract.

- Make sure realistic budgets cover 3 stages – D&C, commissioning completion and transition into steady-state operations; first 2 years of operations.
- The Client and the Concessionaire (commonly called the SPC – Special Purpose Company) must know the Contract documents inside out and backwards, which is not easy, and should educate the subcontractors in understanding the contracts and the obligations and risk transfers contained within them.

Establishing the Project Leadership and Team Spirit

- Must have strong SPC leadership that starts the project positively and proactively manages all key areas.
- Ensure effective communications and stakeholder relationship management; the SPC should be the point of liaison for all stakeholders by overviewing everything and ensuring relevant parties are never left out of the loop, by having all documents pass strictly through the SPC, but be careful not to be viewed as only a "post box".
- Negative communications can be very damaging – watch out for "silent assassins".
- SPC to be the leader with reporting; expediting programs; resolving issues; public relations; stakeholder relationship building (entertainment, etc.).

Agree the Key Processes with all stakeholders at the outset

- The SPC needs to quickly put in place all the processes mentioned in Chapter 14 (Structuring Projects) and to get all stakeholders to buy into them.

Construction Phase

- Design development lead time – don't start construction too soon on site to "make an impression".
- PPP User Groups – firmly reject unreasonable "Xmas Wish-list" shopping by the Client and/ or User Groups during detailed design development – to adjudicate this is an SPC leadership role. The issue is that at this stage the Project Agreement has been signed and the Contractor has a finite contract sum to work within. To do this requires good value engineering, with 'horse trading' and 'give and take' to maintain the cost base and budgets – and it is very important that the FM subcontractor is fully involved.
- Maintain budgets and stay cost neutral through give-and-take value engineering, especially with equipment in hospitals.
- Value engineering is the key to maintaining the Contractor's margins, and the client's contract allowances, e.g. equipment procurement – it is often necessary for the client to relinquish something in order to get something else.
- Cost-neutral solutions keep everyone happy.
- Equipment choice procurement, with client selection (can be a tricky area, keeping everyone happy and maintaining the budget).
- Make sure the Services Provider (FM) endorses all drawings and equipment purchases so they cannot complain later.
- 'Fitness for Intended Purpose' (FFIP) or 'functionality' – contractual obligations in respect of FFIP can be a trap if these obligations are not clearly spelt out in the Contract, because if not it leaves the door open for the client/operator to make unreasonable demands on the basis that *'it does not meet fitness for the intended purpose'*, which can become very subjective.
- Constantly monitor progress v program; costs v budget; and construction quality – be a step ahead of the independent technical inspectors – you don't want the banks asking about something you should have reported.
- Don't let it become a *"remote"* site – the Client's contract is with the SPC and that is where he will call first – and the SPC being right on top of the construction and FM activities will pre-empt any short-cutting or lack of input; it will also ensure the earliest possible knowledge of issues and hopefully make it easier to resolve them.

- Vital ingredient for success – the Contractor must have an effective QA system that ensures that User Group *"agreements"* are all picked up in the drawings or equipment schedules and incorporated in the construction, even before the amendments are re-issued – nothing annoys a Client more than having to take the QA role by default through sloppiness in the design management.
- Major Modifications/Variations – stick to the process in the Contract – generally the Client has to pay for design and estimating – be careful of doing favours by providing estimates for *'maybe variations'*, which they invariably request to save money – they have a habit of backfiring.
- Also, Contractors should be careful to not put in rip-off prices because they think they have a captive client; it is a great way to damage the relationship and make it twice as hard to get genuine variations approved – the SPC leadership should jump right on this.
- Be very prompt with all contractual correspondence – efficiency builds upon itself.
- Modifications and Variations are regular causes of trouble and damage to relationships.

Commissioning, completion and transition to operations

- Single biggest issue in PPP projects around the world – contractors do not allow enough time for commissioning – very different to normal D&C projects, which traditionally might only be 95% finished at Practical Completion and the remainder is completed during the Defects Liability period.
- The SPC needs to engage a highly experienced Transition Manager to liaise with and coordinate the activities of all parties – at an early stage – say one year from completion – not the same as a Commissioning Manager, who is supplied by the contractor.
- Ideally, all Stakeholders contribute to the cost of the Transition Manager – but difficult to achieve sometimes.
- Use a Deed of Variation and an Amending Instrument to formally document all amendments to the Contract, Specifications and the scope of Services that have taken place during design development and construction in order to reduce risk at the start of operations. It makes the client focus on reviewing and checking detailed architectural and services drawings and equipment schedules. Can be difficult getting Clients to agree to Amending Instruments as they feel they are giving away risk transfer – arguments in favour are:
  - This is what the User Groups want – so lock it in
  - Staff will change – don't want expensive disputes with new staff that will damage the good relationship
  - Risk still lies with the Contractor for the facility to be 'fit for intended purpose' (FFIP), but is reduced
  - Original Brief will be obsolete – Royal Women's Hospital in Melbourne had over 700 design and equipment changes – they need to be accurately recorded and signed-off by the Stakeholders
  - Better to do the hard work on agreeing the detail now

- **With the facilities management,** remember that:
  - Thorough training = management competence
  - Management competence = no abatements (efficient preventative maintenance, use of cure plans, etc.)
  - Understanding this = reduced risk priced into Bids
  - Remember that with constantly changing staff, with both the Facilities Manager and the Client, it is important to build into the contracts on-going structured, regular training and accreditation courses

Defects liability period

- Management of defects – a major issue with PPP projects, especially hospitals and prisons, is that it is necessary to be 99.9% defect free at PC, for two reasons:

○ The Independent Tester will require it

○ Access for fixing defects will be restricted as soon as the facility goes into the operations phase

- Use of *'task teams'* – much more efficient and overall more economical for everyone, because coordinating subcontractors is difficult; they are careless and damage the work of others without a care in the world. A typical task team consists of a supervisor from the contractor and one skilled tradesperson from each of the main subcontractors involved in the completion and commissioning, e.g. an electrician, plumber, painter, furniture joiner, IT technician, etc. The team works its way sequentially through rooms and corridors, fixing all defects (snags in the UK) and locking the rooms off as they proceed. Contractors should make *'task teams'* a mandatory procedure because it is a *'win-win'* for everyone – and it is really good risk management.

- Managing defects rectification becomes complicated and requires an Interface Agreement between the Contractor and the FM Subcontractor, with the FM Subcontractor being responsible for all but major items involving Warranties, such as large equipment breakdown. If not handled this way there is unnecessary exposure to abatement risk.

- It is far less expensive and more efficient to rectify defects before PC – just ensure there is enough time in the program.

Claims and disputes

- Remember that the Client contractually only has direct contract with the SPC in a PPP, not with the Contractor and the Facilities Manager, even though the subcontracts form part of the Project Agreement.

Summary of Key Factors for Success and Minimizing Risk

- Know your Contract – Contractors have a bad habit of never reading the Project Agreement
- Provide strong leadership in all areas, especially communications and stakeholder relationships
- Always engage the Facilities Manager (sometimes called the Services Provider) early in the process, right from the start of the Bid
- Establish effective management platforms for document control, activities schedules, etc.
- Ensure that cost planning and design development work closely together
- Ensure that all project documentation, correspondence, minutes, claims and variations, programs and schedules of key activities and key issues, etc. are kept up to date on a daily basis
- Manage issues proactively – *"talk first – write later"*
- Closely monitor progress v. program and cost-to-complete v. budget
- Be on top of the risk management – *"anticipate, anticipate, anticipate"*

**Successful PPPs reflect the human dynamics working
properly in all areas for all stakeholders**

Hypothetical Issues to Test PPP Contract Documents

Notes:

The following contractual issues are based on real issues that occurred in two different hospital PPPs and they could well apply to other similar projects. They show how unexpected and quite complex contractual situations can arise, despite the best efforts by all concerned to structure the contracts as tightly as possible to try and cover all possibilities.

The answers are not being provided, but the objective is to provide readers with thought-provoking ideas that might be helpful when conducting due diligence on new contracts. It is useful to create your own difficult situations to test the contracts.

To determine the liability arising with these issues, it is important to cross-reference the four principal contracts and not look at any one of them in isolation (Project Agreement, Finance Agreement, D&C Contract and FM Services Contract). Often this is difficult and it is necessary to flow-chart your way through the risk transfers

Proving liability must be done by clearly stated contract references, including those from each contract, the specifications and departmental bulletins on standards, if there is an order of precedence involved.

1. A User Group specifies 6 beds plus other furniture in a ward. After installation it is found that the ward is too crowded and does not comply with the disabled access code.

   Who is responsible for the necessary changes and cost?

2. After PC it is discovered that the site boundaries plan provided by the Dept. during bidding was wrong and the car park has to be extended at a cost of $1.0 m. The Dept. denies liability, saying the SPC and the Contractor were responsible for checking the survey, irrespective.

   Do the SPC or the Contractor have a contractual obligation to extend the car park, and if so on what basis?
   If extended, who is responsible for the cost?

3. The joint-sealing method for the coving in the showers meets the specs as signed-off, but shortly before PC the Dept. anti-infection inspector rejects the joints for not meeting the Code. PC is delayed three weeks as a result.

   Who is responsible for the necessary changes and cost, including the delay?

4. Global Brands theatre pendants Model xyz were ordered at a cost of $3.0 m., as agreed with the User Group. There is a change of Clinical Head during construction and after installation the new Head says the model was superseded two years ago and he demands the pendants be replaced because new techniques cannot be used with the ones installed. The cost to replace them is $3.5 m.

   Who is responsible for the change and cost?

5. The new pendants are installed and there is another change of Clinical Head just before PC. He is only 5ft tall and says the pendants have to be extended because they are not fit for purpose and do not comply with H&S regulations for his use. The cost is $1.0 m. plus 3 weeks delay of PC.

   Who is responsible for the change and cost, including the delay?

6. The FM Services Co. under-priced the life cycle because they relied on a schedule given to them by the Contractor during bidding. The schedule they were given did not comply with the Dept. standard. The Contractor recognized this after FC and installed the compliant equipment, at an extra cost of $1.0 m.

   Who is responsible for the extra life cycle cost?

7. The FM Services Co. did not attend some design coordination meetings, despite being invited, and did not comment on drawings tabled and subsequently signed-off for construction. After installation it was found that access to a considerable number of rodding points is difficult, although not impossible. FM Services Co., supported by the hospital administrators, object strongly and demand a change, at a cost of $1.0 m. including delay time.

   Who is responsible for the change and cost, including the delay?

8. During some demolition (or ground works) that takes place after the contract start date, as agreed in the signed-off program, asbestos (or ground contamination) was found that was not expected and causes a 2-month delay.

   Who is responsible for the resultant costs, including the delay?

9. An obscure Health Dept. regulation is contained in a document not mentioned anywhere in the Contracts and Specifications. Just before PC it is discovered and the Dept. insists it is a mandatory standard. The cost of the changes is $1.0 m.

   Who is responsible for the resultant costs, including any delay?

10. An item of Global Brands x-ray equipment is nominated in the 3 principal contract documents and the Health Dept. standards bulletin, but with one different digit in the six digit model number stated in each document; i.e. there are four models, all similar and catering for the same purpose but with different options. A dispute arises because the Dept., the Contractor and the FM Services Co. all want supply of a different model, at different prices.

   What is the precedence of documents?

11. Four hours before Financial Close the Dept. verbally agrees to delete $2.0 m. of equipment at procurement cost, plus the consequent life cycle value, in order to meet affordability, but because of the frantic activity this was not documented, except for some schedules that were used to calculate the values. These were not included in the Contracts. Six months later this omission was discovered, but the Dept. now denies liability, saying the Specs as written in the Contract must stand. The Contractor and the FM Services Co. say the SPC is liable, and the SPC says the Dept. is liable.

   Where does the liability stand?

12. Some rooms are specified to have mechanical ventilation and heating to provide a range of 20-23 degrees C. In a section of the M&E Specification there is one sentence that says that if this temperature range cannot be achieved because the equipment and personnel numbers in the rooms generate too much heat load, then the Contractor must provide an air conditioning system that can achieve this range.

   It fails and the Contractor makes the change, at an increased procurement cost. The life cycle implications are significant and will cost the FM Services Co. $10.0 m. at NPV. They say they did not see the single sentence in the large Spec; they were not alerted to it at any time; the Contract documents are not clear about the amount of equipment and allowable personnel numbers; and they did not allow for the possibility of this extra life cycle cost. The Dept. and the SPC deny liability and say it falls with the FM Services Co. They sue everyone, including the Contractor.

Who is liable?

13. The FM Services Co. will run their operations and monitor the BMS from a central control room. For some inexplicable reason this control room is not mentioned anywhere in the contract documents or on any contract drawings. The Contractor denies liability and the SPC says it is an implied term of the Building Contract because it is obvious a modern hospital cannot be operated without a control room.

Who is liable for the cost of installing the room, together with the M&E required?

Structuring Projects – the different stages, activities and responsibilities from concept to completion of construction

Before analysing particular risks and why projects fail, it is important to understand the bigger picture of how projects are structured and in doing so identify the main areas for potential risk.

Essentially, responsibility for risk management is spread amongst the main participants in a project, irrespective of whether the project is conducted as a Lump Sum contract, a D&C contract, a PPP contract, or a Cost Plus contract (a dangerous way for a client to live!), or some other form. There are always two parties to the contract and between them they have to manage the risks carefully in order to deliver a successful project. This includes taking responsibility for their subcontractors.

The following processes and procedures typically occur in most construction projects, although not all of them in every project. For example most of the processes listed below will apply to PPP projects, but not all of them to a construction-only project. PPPs have far more potential risks and I have commented on them in Chapter 13.

What is important is that if any of the following processes are not properly established and efficiently managed then the project will be put at serious risk of failure to some degree or other. **And all these processes are implemented by people, so that is your number one risk.** This is why many successful construction companies insist on key decisions being signed off by two senior people.

The parties responsible for the following processes are identified in italics: *(client, contractor, user/ operator, facilities manager (FM))*

Structuring the project *(client)*

- Concept – the architectural schematic design and the business case
- Client financing – concept stage and whole of project
- Site acquisition
- Planning and other authority approvals
- Feasibility studies
- Preparation for tender – assessing the overall project; the common sense of the concept
- Assessing the degree of readiness to proceed
- The Client's own resources and competency
- The political situation
- Calling for Expressions of Interest (EOI's) and planning the tender

Tendering and Bidding Activities *(client, contractor, user/operator, FM)*

With traditional contracts it is essentially the responsibility of the client to manage the process, but with D&C and PPP projects there is also substantial involvement from the contractor, the future operator and the facilities manager.

- Preparing the tender documents – drawings, specifications, special terms and conditions
- Design development and cost planning in parallel for D&C and PPP projects
- Establishing the risk management process
- Consideration of operational items – end-user requirements, O&M, life cycle replacement
- D&C planning and programming
- Firming up prices – subcontractors and suppliers

- Bid qualifications
- Due diligence on Contract documents
- Client check of financial strength and experience of all participants in the Bid (should have occurred during assessment of EOI's)

Establishing the Risk Management Process

(Each party is responsible for their own risk management)

- The extent to which this is done will depend on the size of the project, but at the very least a Risk Management Schedule should be prepared that covers all areas of the project. Large projects should appoint a specific Risk Manager whose task it will be to consolidate and monitor all of the potential risks that are nominated up-front by the different section managers. Refer to Chapter 20 for further elaboration on this point and a typical team structure and flow chart for controlling risks.

Finalising the Financing and the Contract

- Establish realistic and carefully prepared budgets and cash flow projections for progress claims and milestone payments *(client, contractor)*
- Have a realistic Contract sum analysis and scheduled rates for overheads, preliminaries and margins, *(contractor)*
- Agree fixed margins in the Contract for modifications/variations for the contractor, facilities manager and equity partner in the case of PPPs, so that arguments over future variations are minimised *(client, contractor)*
- Ensure the financial structure has some flexibility and headroom for variations *(client)*
- When preparing PPP contracts, place heavy concentration on the services scope and obligations in the Contract Schedules *(client)*
- Test the Contract as much as possible to eliminate black holes, grey areas and ambiguities *(client, contractor)*

Establishing the Project Leadership and Team Spirit

Early appointments of a top-line project director *by all the main stakeholders*

Establish and demonstrate real leadership from the outset, through a Stakeholder Workshop held immediately after signing the Contract, or Financial Close for PPPs *(client):*

- To establish relationships, relationship management and guiding behaviours
- Commence building trust and respect
- Understand the needs and success factors of all stakeholders
- Establish common goals; agree key objectives and mission statements
- e.g. *"A World Model PPP"* & *"No Disputes"*
- Generate positive attitudes and create team spirit

Run Review Workshops at least every 6 months – main things that need "renewal" will be relationships, communications protocols and project objectives – remember that staff changes are always happening *(client).*

Agree the Key Processes with all stakeholders at the outset

- Control and Reporting requirements and procedures – Client, Project or SPC manager, Contractor, Design Consultants, FM
- Management and document control platforms with different levels of access, e.g. Team Binder, Incite, SharePoint

PROJECT CRISIS - INTERNAL RAPID ESCALATION PLAN

Level 1 Incident
INSIGNIFICANT

An incident that is:
- A hazard identified/near-miss situation with no harm and not likely to generate media interest.

Level 2 Incident
MINOR

An incident that:
- Is likely to generate some general, low level media interest, with local press, TV and radio, e.g. within a 50 km radius

Level 3 Incident
MODERATE

An incident (with no loss of life) that:
- Is likely to generate strong media interest, with national press, TV and radio; and
- Requires timely, accurate, credible and consistent communications; and
- Threatens the reputation/public image of the SPC and equity holders, the Authority Concession Partner and the State, and/or other internal Stakeholders.

Level 4 Incident
MAJOR

An incident (with loss of life) that:
- Might involve the active and ongoing involvement of emergency services agencies at a provincial & national level;
- Is likely to generate strong media interest;
- Requires timely, accurate, credible and consistent communications; and
- Threatens the reputation/public image of the SPC and equity holders, the Authority Concession Partner and the State, and/or other internal Stakeholders.

SPCs to agree a Media Communications Protocol with Partners, with specific guidelines, e.g.
- All media enquiries referred to the Gov't Partner; or
- Report on facts only
- Consult internal specialists first, etc

Flowchart

Incident First Awareness

Immediate Communication between Stakeholders

- Client Operations
- FM Service Provider

SPC Management → SPC Assessment of Crisis

Level 1 Incident INSIGNIFICANT
SPC Manager's responsibility - no rapid escalation required - note in monthly Report

Level 2 Incident MINOR
IMMEDIATE REGIONAL ESCALATION
- SPC Manager or Project Staff
- SPC Directors & Regional Ops Dir/Asset Mng
- Regional CEO & Legal Services

Level 3 Incident MODERATE

Level 4 Incident MAJOR

IMMEDIATE HIGH LEVEL ESCALATION
- SPC Manager or Project Staff
- SPC Directors & Regional Ops Dir/Asset Mng
- Regional CEO & Legal Services
- International MD's Board M's, Corp PR Mng, Dir Asset M

NAME	POSITION	EMERGENCY NUMBERS
	SPC Manager	
	SPC Directors	
	Ops Director	
	Reg Asset Mng	
	Regional CEO	
	Internat. MD's	
	Board Members	
	Corp PR Mng	
	Dir Asset M	

- Communications protocols – establish clear rules – no side-plays
- Meetings and Working Groups – strict rules – with timetables, mandatory attendances, agendas, delivery times for Minutes – chaired and proactively led by project directors
- HS&E regimes
- Crisis management planning (see more details at the end of this chapter)

Construction Phase *(contractor, FM)*

- Financing, staffing and allocation of resources
- Org charts and job descriptions
- Planning and programming
- Detailed design development, again in parallel with the cost plan
- Full involvement of the FM from Day-1 – "whole of life"; O&M practicality and optimisation; *'granite can be cheaper than bricks over 25 years'*

Commissioning, completion and transition to operations *(Client, contractor, user/operator, FM)*

- Ensure enough time is allowed for commissioning and provide adequate resources – PPPs can take far more time and resources than normal D&C projects, which traditionally might only be 95% finished at Practical Completion and the remainder is completed during the Defects Liability period (see Chapter 13 on PPPs)
- It is a common error to cut short on resources and the time allowed when budgeting, but this can prove expensive in the long run
- Program the activities carefully, with participation and agreement from all stakeholders, particularly the client, user/operator and the facilities manager who will take over full control during the transition period
- Do not confuse completion, commissioning and transition. Treat them as entirely separate activities and plan, program and resource them accordingly
- Experienced Commissioning and Transition Managers should be engaged – the Transition Manager's role is to liaise with and coordinate the activities of all stakeholders and is not the same as the Commissioning manager, who comes from the contractor

Defects liability period *(client, contractor, FM)*

- Plan and program the management and resourcing for the rectification of the defects in conjunction with the relevant subcontractors
- PPP projects, hospitals and prisons in particular, are more difficult than traditional construction or D&C projects as it is necessary to be 99.9% defect free at PC, for two reasons:
  - The Independent Tester will require it under the Contract
  - Access for fixing defects will be restricted as soon as the facility goes into the operations phase
- Form subcontractor *'task teams'* for an efficient rectification process
- An Interface Agreement should be in place between the contractor and the facilities manager, with the FM being responsible for all but major items involving Warranties, such as large equipment breakdown
- It can be cost effective for the contractor to subcontract the management of the defects rectification to the FM after the bulk of the defects have been fixed

Claims and disputes *(all parties)*

- Establish clear methodologies in the Contract and in the early stakeholder working sessions for reviewing and processing claims. Stick to strict time schedules for processing claims, because they only get harder the longer they are left
- Ensure that the Contract includes a workable Dispute Resolution section. All too often this is left to the last minute and something is included in a rush without proper thought

- In structuring the Dispute Resolution process, ensure that there is an emphasis on negotiated settlements, with plenty of opportunity for this to take place
- With D&C and PPP projects encourage the parties to adopt value engineering "trade-offs" when design and equipment changes take place during design development, with the objective being a cost neutral result. This is a good way of minimizing potential future disputes over variations

Crisis Management Planning *(all parties)*

A crisis on a construction site is very much a human behavioural situation and you can never be sure how people will react under the stress of a crisis.

It is important that each project establishes procedures at the outset for Crisis Management and Crisis Communications and that everyone working on the site or connected with the project through one of the stakeholders is inducted into the procedures.

The two crisis procedures, management and communications, are equally important; e.g. if there is a serious accident on a site the treatment and evacuation of the injured person has paramount importance, but at the same time it is essential to communicate details of the incident promptly and in the right manner to the family of the injured person and to the CEO's of the construction company, the client and subcontractors that are involved, because the last thing you want is for them to hear about it first from a reporter or on the TV news.

There are a number of potential crises that can occur on a project and procedures should be developed to handle these different areas of risk.

The following *'Internal Rapid Escalation Plan'* is a typical crisis communication plan for stakeholders, which can be extended to cover the media and the community.

Understanding and Managing Contracts

The way in which contracts are written, understood and managed can have a huge impact on the progress and efficient delivery of a construction project.

It is amazing how people can take a relatively straight-forward contract document and turn it into one which contains terms that are ambiguous and difficult to understand and has grey areas or gaping black holes in respect of the rights and obligations of the parties. It is important to minimise these areas of risk when drafting contracts and during the subsequent due diligence by the parties prior to signing. The parties to the contract normally work closely in conjunction with their lawyers during the drafting phase.

During the drafting, due diligence and checking stages with a contract it is a good idea to have the hands-on project managers to test the contract with some difficult hypothetical situations (see chapter 13 in this regard).

It is really helpful to project managers and others administering the contract, such as the quantity surveyors, if the Terms of Contract are written as much as possible in layman's language and not in convoluted 'lawyer-speak'. Fortunately there has been considerable improvement in this direction in recent years. Likewise, there has been considerable improvement in the general format of contracts, as discussed by Rob Horne in chapter 16.

It is also important to not have too many cross-references in the Terms, both within the main contract and between related contracts, as with PPPs where you have a suite of contracts, such as the Project Agreement, the Finance Agreement, the Construction Contract and the Facilities Management Contract. Some contracts have so many cross-references that you have to flow-chart your way through the documents to find out whom is responsible for what in respect of the rights and obligations of the parties. A simple clause in the Construction Contract may just refer to the Project Agreement, but that particular Term may have serious ramifications for the Contractor in regard to pass-through obligations to provide facilities and be responsible for the costs thereof; similarly with the Facilities Manager and their obligations down the track.

When it comes to implementing the contract, project managers cannot do this efficiently if they do not fully understand all the Terms, Conditions and Specifications and the rights and obligations flowing from them. Managers need to know and understand the Terms of Contract so well that they know immediately where to look for any given situation.

It is then equally important that project managers carefully comply with the documentation requirements of the contract, as distinct to the technical delivery of the specifications and the program. They must also carefully comply with the processes related to administration, such as with the content and time limits for Notices, Variations and Extensions of Time. Failure to do so can be a very expensive oversight.

Contracts that are well drafted should be beneficial for both parties and provide the framework for a smooth project delivery, with minimal extra costs and disputed issues, subject to each party managing the contract efficiently and complying with their obligations.

In the next two chapters Rob Horne and Graham Thomson comprehensively address how to draft, understand and manage construction contracts and the associated risks.

77

Effective Contract Writing to Minimise Construction Disputes

By Rob Horne, International Construction Lawyer
Chartered Arbitrator and Adjudicator

Why is a self-confessed dispute resolution lawyer writing on the subject of effective contract drafting? Let me say from the outset, I have not drafted a full construction contract in very many years[1]. How can I then add anything of relevance to this issue? Well, most disputes in construction projects revolve around how well the contractual documentation, drafted at the outset before work has even begun on site, has reacted to the challenges of the project. Therefore, what I am hoping to add in this chapter is not an explanation of what is "bad drafting" in the sense of sentence structure and choice of words. Rather I am going to consider the principles that should guide the drafting and I do that from looking backwards from a dispute or issues occurring on a project to its root cause.

Far too often in situations where dispute or conflict feels inevitable the apt, though overused, phrase *"I wouldn't start from here"* can be heard. While this may be apt, and indeed is almost certainly a truism, it helps very little with the problem the parties to a project find themselves in. However, following the thread back through the life of the project can lead to some surprising insights into the root of the problem. What may have started as a simple, well intentioned, innocent looking piece of drafting in the Boardroom[2] can looking remarkably different midway through a project. Looked at from the project end of the telescope effective contract drafting is often viewed very differently to how it was viewed while being prepared and agreed.

Equally, it is tempting, when considering contract drafting, to consider only the lead construction contract. However, as will become obvious on analysis, this is far too narrow a focus. The whole supply network needs to be considered from employer to designer, to subcontractor to supplier. Any break in the commonality of the drafting within the supply network will increase, rather than minimise, the chances of disputes occurring[3].

While it might be tempting to look just to the drafting of the words on the page, point the finger, and says *"there's your problem; you wrote X in your agreement when you meant Y"* that is, regrettably, a vast over simplification. Who wrote those words? Why were they written that way? How do they fit in with the rest of the project documentation?[4] How are they understood at a project as well as at Boardroom level? Stopping at the words on the page, while certainly what a lawyer will do to reach a legal answer to a specific question, is not the route to solving the "don't start from here" dilemma and neither is it the mechanism through which problems on future projects can be solved. Neither, of course will it even begin to deal with perhaps the greater evil, and almost always the *"elephant in the room"* that nobody thought to look to the contract until there was a problem, by which time it was probably to late to minimise and avoid and the parties were forced to resolve.

---

[1]Although I do conduct training on the meaning and application of certain standard forms and I am often asked for my view on the effectiveness of certain terms and provisions within the overall drafting exercise

[2]Throughout I use "Boardroom" for the senior management of the contracting parties whose job it is to enter into the project documentation but not carry out the detailed delivery of the project

[3]There are very few true multi—party construction contracts but see the PPC2000 form of contract as an example of such an approach

[4]I do not say the contract documents here as that would be to over simplify the background to how contract documents are arrived at and is a topic I shall return to

While this paper may be an exploration of the idea of drafting to avoid disputes it is within a much larger context of considering and understanding the human dynamic which underpins and drives projects from inception, through drafting to delivery.

The written words are meaningless without human interaction to bring them to life and give them meaning. In particular, the words have to be operated and adhered to otherwise, no matter how good (or indeed bad) the drafting it will play no part in minimising the risk of a dispute. Therefore, while going through some common issues that arise and exploring the idea of drafting to avoid disputes, it is the much larger context of considering and understanding the human dynamic which underpins and drives projects from inception, through drafting to delivery.

The written words are meaningless without human interaction to bring them to life and give them meaning. In particular, the words have to be operated and adhered to otherwise, no matter how good (or indeed bad) the drafting, it will play no part in minimising the risk of a driving the potential problem, dispute and solution should become apparent.

A good place to start is with a hypothesis; you may agree, or not, the purpose is to shape the discussion and deepen the understanding. So the hypothesis here is that there are just six key or principle issues which drive problems with drafting to minimise disputes. Those six are like the ingredients of a cake, if one is missing or not quite right the cake, as a whole, won't be quite right. It can be difficult to identify what was missing unless you have significant expertise, however the result is plain to see. The six principles, or ingredients, to minimising disputes through contract drafting are:

1. **Common Understanding** (or lack thereof) – Particularly with regard to project outputs - what a successful project will look like, and project inputs – what is needed to create the output. The lack of understanding could be on the part of any or all of the project parties and the further out of alignment the understanding is the more likely a dispute is to occur. Recording this common understanding is one of the key purposes of a contract but one which often gets overtaken by the detail of specifications and the like.

2. **Clarity** – Having understood what the project is about, the way that understanding is recorded needs to be clear and unambiguous. This is the issue which is most readily associated with drafting, often to the exclusion of the other principles identified and described here leading to over simplification and a significantly reduced chance to avoid the "don't start from here" scenario. Clarity does come from appropriate use of words and sentence structures but if it is not properly linked back to the first principle, common understanding, then it will inevitably fail to be clear no matter good the individual words used.

3. **Knowledge transfer** – It would be nice to think that a set of words can mean the same thing to all those who read them?[5] Unfortunately, experience shows that this is not the case. Even where there has been good understanding and clarity at Boardroom level when it comes to detailed implementation of the project that knowledge needs to be transferred effectively. Therefore, a key part of the drafting exercise, if it is to minimise disputes, is its transmission from Boardroom theory to site operation.

4. **Adaptability** – Every project is different and bespoke in some way, some more so than others, and major projects are often completely unique, one of a kind, builds stretching the boundaries of engineering and architecture?[6] There are a great many unforeseen and even unforeseeable events which occur on construction projects and therefore layered on top of the understanding, clarity and knowledge transfer must be an element of adaptability. This is one of the great balancing acts; achieving adaptability without taking away from clarity.

---

[5]This certainly seems to be the Utopian world that many lawyers live in
[6]See Chapter 9, giving a history of the Sydney Opera House

5. **Acceptance** – One way or another, whatever the contract says needs to be accepted. It is extremely unhelpful, but all too common, for one party, during the construction phase, to think to itself (and on accession say to the other party) "these terms are not fair, we need to change them or abandon them". Such wholesale changes can be extremely effective but only if there is an acceptance of the original terms and therefore who is making what concession.

6. **Application** – The final principle here is that the terms must actually be applied and adhered to. There are innumerable projects, and indeed construction professionals when considering the human dynamic, that rely on putting the contract "in the drawer" and only retrieving it to deal with problems after they have arisen. For the purpose of this discussion (and almost certainly in a general sense as well) that is not application. Proper and timely application must be considered part of drafting as the way in which a contract is written will, to a large extent, define whether it is a useable tool to help guide the parties or a weaponised rulebook only used after the event to try and make a point.

All of these principles, to a greater or lesser extent, can be guided by effective drafting of the contract. The contract is after all, the record of the agreed rights and obligations between the parties and therefore the "answer" to most, if not all, questions should either be in the contract or capable of inference from the contract.

How do these key issues manifest themselves in projects? Unfortunately it is all too easy to identify examples.

Project Example 1

Middle East Residential Development

5 contractors were employed to construct 200 or so villas each with a mix of 5 different villa types. Each contract was carefully negotiated around a FIDIC standard form of contract. A sixth contractor was employed to undertake the infrastructure work across the project as a whole and this approach was understood by all of the contractors. There was a fairly typical term included requiring all of the contractors to work together and coordinate their works.

Halfway through the build some general problems across the development occurred including sandstorms and a general material shortage, particularly in relation to concrete products. In addition, the infrastructure contractor commenced his work and, unfortunately, because he was the only infrastructure contractor, there was no requirement placed on him to coordinate with others.

The infrastructure contractor therefore identified the best sequence of work for himself and commenced. This had obvious knock on consequence to the villa contractors as they could not access certain areas of the site as roadways were being excavated to install drainage and other services. The shortage of cement based products, because each contractor was under separate contracts and potentially subject to damages for late completion, placed each contractor in competition to secure adequate share of the small supply. Some contractors managed to secure full delivery others received almost nothing. The sandstorms in turn made it very difficult to carry out anything other than precast-concrete works but the short supply magnified the effects of the storms.

On this project the contracts did not provide the answers the parties really needed and disputes (or at least differences) arose. Looking back at the principles identified

---

in this paper, the contracts for this project had reasonable common understanding of the nature of the project but the key element was missing, that a very important factor was going to be the sale of the villas as they became available to provide revenue to the developer.

The contracts were not sufficiently clear, particularly in relation to the interface between the contractors. Knowledge transfer occurred but, because of the limited common understanding and clarity this was inadequate to meet the demands and challenges of the project. The contracts, as drafted, were insufficiently adaptable to deal with the changing circumstances of the project which, while extreme, could have been foreseen as possibilities in a project of this complexity. There was little acceptance of the terms of the contracts once the circumstances described occurred, what ensued was a general "blame game" where all parties chose to read their contract in a different way, no matter how strained the interpretation, in order to try and achieve their commercial goal.

Finally, there was insufficient application until the problems were manifest and the parties were reliant on the contract to justify and support the actions they had already taken rather than it being used to formulate and regulate the relationship before either party acted.

When then can parties take steps to improve the drafting of their contracts to minimise disputes? The most obvious starting point (although still lost on some projects) is before they start. If you have already commenced and then try to structure the contract around what you are already doing the risk exposure of the parties is markedly higher. There are, however, occasions when the drafting can be improved after the project has been started but I will return to this shortly as it is easier, and more beneficial, to consider the opportunities in sequence.

Step 1 – Project Inception – This is the very earliest stage at which the kernel of an idea for a project is formed. You could think of it as a *"light-bulb"* moment where someone says *"hey, I've got this great idea…"* However, I prefer to think of it as a *"big bang"* moment. The key difference being that in a *"big bang"* moment, like the formation of the universe, everything about the project in fact crystallises at that moment. You may not realise it, understand it or deal with it yet but all risks and opportunities coalesce in that "big bang" moment. Soon after the initial big bang, ideas will start to be reduced to writing and this is the protean form of contract. It is at this stage that the first cut of opportunities and risks will be considered and it is at this stage that the first of the principles described above is at the fore.

The common understanding will probably start from a set of outputs from the project; what is it we are trying to achieve from this project. Why is this particular formulation better than another? Even though the detail of how those objectives are to be carried into effect will change and develop, properly recording the original objectives is key. With the proper initial objectives recorded development of implementation can be measured against something and there will be an *"essential quality"* of the project around which a common understanding can grow and allow the other principles to be achieved.

Project Example 2

Cambridgeshire Guided Busway

This is a unique piece of infrastructure, being a specialist and dedicated running track for buses only. In Cambridgeshire the route of the busway was to follow an existing but by that time disused railway line from the town of St Ives to the edge of the City of Cambridge where the buses would transition onto bus lanes on conventional roads, and then back on to dedicated guideway to link to the railway station for Cambridge and Addenbrookes hospital.

The *"big bang"* moment was the need for alternative transport into the City of Cambridge and was part of a multi modal study for all transport in and around Cambridge. The big bang reduced into key objectives around speed of transportation, ride quality and accessibility. Consideration was given to numerous ways of achieving these objectives including renewing the railway, constructing a conventional but dedicated road, using a slip-formed concrete guideway or using a pre-cast solution. As the objectives of the route had been thought through at project inception the options were narrowed to a pre-cast concrete guideway and there was an easy and obvious common understanding on the key priorities for the route.

As history has shown, from resultant disputes, particularly with regard to this second project example above, clarity, common understanding and all the other principles being in place at project inception is no guarantee that the project will be dispute free. Equally, the work done at project inception will not amount to effective drafting to minimise disputes; it is just one step on the way to achieve that. There are, at project inception, still many stages at which the drafting can become ineffective at minimising disputes or in fact can positively promote and encourage dispute.

The knowledge transfer and other drafting issues at this stage are focussed on drawing in the professional team to the developer. Beyond project inception, the developer usually takes a step back from the project while the professional team start to add detail. Therefore, if the essential objectives of the project have not been properly recorded, or drafted, at project inception stage the detail of the project will be layered on top of an inadequate foundation and is therefore far more likely to lead to disputes.

Step 2 – Procurement and Tender – Where the project inception step was all about initial ideas and recording them to ensure focus this step is focussed on the initial contact with the team that will take the idea to reality. The key part of this step is that it will define the expectations of both parties. The principles at the forefront here are the creation of a common understanding, now between developer, professional team and constructor, and clarity of those documents that are going to be defining those expectations and requirements.

The temptation of many developers is to hurry through this stage, almost as if it is a necessary evil rather than an important part of the process. The rise, to dominance in many areas, of design and build construction has led to many developers seeing the tender stage as an expenditure to be minimised or avoided as the risk and requirements of bringing the project into reality is going to be passed to the constructor. The most often encountered problem with this is that, once in the build phase, the developer does not like some detail of what is being constructed and therefore seeks to change it. Many developers omit to consider or do not accept that such changes may well lead to unexpected consequences such as additional cost or time to complete.

Northern Ireland Housing Executive - v - Healthy Buildings Limited

This project had a dispute which ended in the Northern Ireland Court of Appeal.

Healthy Buildings were appointed by the Housing Executive to carry out asbestos surveys to various numbers of its housing stock which were being regenerated. The appointment contract required Healthy Buildings to comply with relevant legislation in the carrying out of the investigations and made particular reference to the standard requirements for how investigations were to be carried out. However, the standard allowed for a choice of two different ways of carrying out those surveys; one amounted to a survey by example and the other amounted to a detailed survey of each house to be regenerated. The Housing Executive did not specify which method they preferred or required at tender stage. Just after the contract had been awarded the parties met to discuss implementation. At that stage the Housing Executive made a selection of the method of survey they wanted, preferring the more detailed house by house option.

Unfortunately, as the need had not been communicated clearly and there was no common understanding. Healthy Buildings had priced on the cheaper option. The Housing Executive did not want to pay more as they said it was open to them to choose either option as both had been in the tender documents. Healthy Buildings did not want to carry what would be a considerable loss as they had been led to believe the choice was theirs.

The court found that the choice of one option over another was a change and therefore the Housing Executive was to pay the extra cost. The lack of clarity had left the choice in the hands of Healthy Buildings rather than the Housing Executive.

This step in formulating the eventual contract should add to, strengthen and support the foundation stone laid during the project inception stage. Imagine two foundation blocks working in tandem to support a building; as long as they work in tandem everything that follows should be simple. However, if they are misaligned so they do not produce a single level starting point, or perhaps if they are made of different materials that will react differently when stress is applied to them then the opportunity for a problem has been created. The further out of alignment they are the harder it is to recover, the more substantial the difference in material (even if both materials can be used as a proper foundation on their own) the more likely it is that additional and unexpected stresses will be applied during the project.

Step 3 – Contract negotiations – The discussions and negotiations that occur around and during the tender period allow alternative views to be put and an opportunity is created for additional benefit to be added by the constructor. The increased use of two stage tendering, where one stage is competitive and then there is a second stage with a preferred bidder where more ideas and opportunities can be explored, certainly promotes the importance of this stage[7].

The key principle at play during this stage is clarity but also with a healthy dose of knowledge transfer and a deepening of the common understanding. To achieve these three principles the discussions and drafting being produced at this stage needs to be done in as open a way as possible if disputes are to be avoided. Unfortunately, it is often at exactly this stage that the paths of constructor, developer and professional team can easily diverge.

During this step everything is starting to get quite "real" and the tendency for many parties is to look to their own interests first. Indeed, why wouldn't that be the case? The developer will either have public accountability if it is public body or will be answerable to shareholders if private. Equally, the constructor, who will probably working on a very tight margin[8], is carrying out the works for reward, in other words he needs to make a profit. The professional team will have significant influence and control over the constructor but will not, generally, be answerable to the constructor. The natural instinct of all parties is to protect their own interests first. In doing so, that protection will often not be through an open dialogue until each party think they understand the risk they are taking and look for opportunity to minimise the risk they carry and maximise the opportunity from risk carried by others.

It is rare for there to be a fully open joint examination of the risk inherent in the project as a whole, such discussions, when they occur, tend to focus on specific aspect of the project or particular issues which have arisen during the discussions to that point. If one were to look for a single point at which the preparation and drafting of contracts most often goes astray or stops being about minimising the chance of future problems, it is this step in the process.

---

[7] For additional information see, for example, "Early Contractor Involvement in Building Procurement: Contracts, Partnering and Project Management" by David Mosey.

[8] A profit margin, and therefore risk margin, for a general contracting company in the UK could be expected to be from 1%-5% and that profit margin will usually be expected to absorb any risk the constructor cannot mitigate while on site

---

Project Example 4

Design Appointment on a Design and Build Project

This was a project for the construction of a road in the UK. A fairly challenging timetable was set but the constructor had appointed a designer to assist it during the tender stage The contractor won the work on the basis of a lump sum price and fixed completion date set out in a detailed programme.

The detailed construction programme included dates for design release and activities for carrying out work on site following the release of those designs. The activities flowed logically through the project from one to another through to completion within the contractual limit. The logic within the programme linking activities together and creating a dynamic model for the project was sound and allowed for good management of the activities and clear forecasting of progress.

What was missing was support to that programme from others in the supply network, in particular the designer. The designer had provided a confirmation that it would provide design in order to allow the activities in the constructors programme to be achieved. While this was acceptable as a statement it did not provide sufficient clarity to anyone on the project once site activities commenced and sequencing started to change. What became apparent very early on in the project was that the constructor was not sufficiently managing the designer to ensure designs were available, in an approved state, in time to allow construction to proceed without interruption.

There was clearly a good common understanding of what was needed but clarity and knowledge transfer had been lost. This cascaded into a failure by the parties to accept the very simple design programme intent and removed any adaptability from the build and from the contract, despite having a "partnering charter" signed by all of the parties.

Step 4 – Contract Execution – Although many would see this as not really a step in the drafting of a contract it is a crucial moment for a number of reasons. First, it is the last chance to get things right in the drafting before rights and responsibilities become locked. Second, this is the key point at which knowledge transfer comes to the fore as the lawyers will step away from the contract at this point and leave it to the parties to implement it. Finally, there is a real danger that this is the step at which the parties believe that the contract has been *"locked"* and therefore they can put it away and not look at it again unless there is a problem, at which point they imagine it will, miraculously, provide an answer acceptable to everyone.

Most of the PFI or PPP projects I have had any involvement with tend to run contract execution up to 11.50pm or so on the day by which contracts must be signed or the funding arrangements will fall away or some equally dire consequence occur. In those last hours there is some very hard, close scrutiny of the project documentation. However, it is highly unlikely that the focus of attention in such projects is on the risky part of actually building something; far more often the key focus is the functioning of the financial model. That is not necessarily a bad thing, I raise the point because the financial model is the real driving force behind the whole project and yet it is being considered, in detail, right up to the last possible moment. When you compare and contrast that to the position in a normal, employer funded, project it is unlikely that such focus is brought to bear on the relevant construction documents. Either they are agreed well in advance or, just as often, they are left over with work commencing under a letter of intent on the assumption that the construction contract will be entered into at some point. With such lack of attention one cannot blame the drafting if there is a problem later, it was never really given a chance.

Perhaps of greater significance however to the project outcome is what happens in the immediate aftermath of contract execution. Most of those involved with drafting the contract, preparing and submitting tender documents and negotiating on particular issues will step away. It is at this moment that many problems with the contract drafting will crystallise. Those problems are not necessarily manifest problems with the drafting itself but simply that the way it has been considered and approached during the tender and up to execution is re-reviewed as the implementation of the project starts and the theory of what, until then, has been a sterile contract is put into practice. The knowledge transfer that needs to occur at this point is critical to success. You may think this has little to do with the contract drafting and, in a traditional sense that might be correct. However, challenging the traditional approach, why isn't the contract drafted properly in the expectation that it is to be implemented and applied by others[9].

Step 5 – Build Phase Implementation (stress testing) – Although a contract has been entered into and fully executed the importance of drafting does not stop there. There are a further two key aspects to consider and at this step the principles of adaptability and acceptance become key.

The first of the two key aspects is the stress testing of the words written into the contract, how they are used and followed, how well they stand up to the scrutiny and challenge of a live project with changing facts and circumstances. The stress testing will focus significantly on the principles of adaptability and acceptance. However, this step can be crippled before it begins if common understanding, clarity and knowledge transfer have not been put in place through earlier stages of the drafting process.

---

[9]This is the precise point made by the NEC for form of contract which is deliberately drafted for implementation on site by engineers rather than for legal review by lawyers. This creates a second tension as the contract still needs to be legally enforceable but it is perhaps a step in the right direction to properly appreciate the reality of how the contract is used

Project Example 5

A PFI Project in the UK

This was a project for the construction of a new hospital with an SPV contracted to the local health authority and a build contractor carrying out the initial work (owned by the main equity holder in the SPV) and an FM contract (who had no interest in the SPV).

During the course of the build phase there were various changes to the room layouts and makeup as well as to how the services were to be provided. The changes being implemented were relatively modest in the build phase but, through the choice of equipment being made by the build contractor, had very substantial repercussions in the operation phase. The majority of the additional build phase costs were fully recoverable whereas the majority if the operational phase costs would end up being borne by the SPV.

The various contracts, despite significant size and complexity, did not provide for this scenario and neither was there sufficient flexibility with the various contract documents to react adequately to this new challenge.

In fact in this project the problem was solved by the SPV equity holder acquiring the FM contractor and therefore being able to balance build and operational risk across the whole project. This is a good example of the human dynamic working to solve a problem.

The second key aspect is change. Practically every construction project will have a degree of change in it; it is an inherent part of the construction process. Whenever change occurs, how that change is recorded and managed should be approached with the same care and diligence as the original contract drafting was. Certainly the same principles as outlined above in relation to the contract itself will be relevant. Unfortunately, it is rare indeed for the same care and attention to be given to change as to the original contract concept, even where the change itself is very significant.

Project Example 6

A Road Project in the Middle East

A project was let for the dualisation of a length of single carriageway road. The project was tendered and a contractor selected and appointed under an amended FIDIC Red Book form of contract. A programme was agreed and a lump sum price was put in place. Within a few months of contract award (on a 30 month project) Variation Order one was issued. Variation Order one provided "add one further lane in each direction to provide a three lane motorway for the length of the project".

With such a significant change the contractor provided a detailed cost and time quotation for this variation. That quote was rejected, but with no alternative suggested. Under the contract the contractor was required to comply with the variation order instructing additional work but had no visibility on the recovery he would make for the additional work. The contract, in any meaningful sense, ceased to operate at that point as the time and money provisions had, effectively, been set aside. The parties continued to negotiate the time and cost implications of the first Variation Order, issued soon after contract award, all the way through to project completion.

Five steps or opportunities in which to align the drafting to minimise the chances of dispute and six principles to consider at each stage, as well as during the transition from one stage to the next. However, is that really enough to understand how to use drafting to minimise the risk of dispute? The reality is that it is and must be. There is little or no point trying to consider what exact form of words will work and what forms will not. While examples can be given of specific instances in which certain terms were inadequate it is likely that there have been many occasions where the same, or very similar, terms have been used without a problem.

Returning to the theme I started with, it is not the particular words that are written down which give rise to the greatest problems. It is how those words are identified and then implemented.

Put simply there is no one right way to draft anything. There is no golden rule that if applied and obeyed will render a project devoid of disputes. This is not surprising as, turning back to the start of this paper, I set out the proposition that it is not the words themselves that create the problem and therefore it would be strange indeed if, not having caused a problem, those same words can act as a miraculous panacea.

The essence of drafting to avoid disputes then is in understanding the human dynamic driving the drafting, how that interaction and knowledge is transferred from Boardroom, legal and tender/procurement team to the project team and then how it is implemented at site to turn words on a page into a functioning project. The drafting, whatever words are chosen, needs to reflect the requirements of the team implementing the project. The drafting needs to be very carefully considered, usually the more time the better, but it needs to be in a context of six principles across five stages, which is as good a starting point as any.

Biography – Rob Horne

Rob is a partner at a leading international law firm, a Chartered Arbitrator and adjudicator who has specialised in finding solutions to construction related problems for over 20 years. He is the author of "The Expert Witness in Construction" published in 2013 and is a recognised expert in the NEC form of contract as well as being an examiner and tutor for both the Chartered Institute of Arbitrators and the Royal Institution of Chartered Surveyors.

Rob's practice is largely based on major projects within the UK and internationally across the Middle East, Africa, Europe and even advising on projects in Australia. He has been involved in disputes up to a value of £250m all tending to be centred around complex engineering problems, significant delay and analysis of disruption caused as a result.

Affinitext – Making Documents Intelligent to Capture Knowledge and Manage Risk & Compliance

By Graham Thomson,
CEO Affinitext Inc.

A clear trend in developed economies is for organisations in both the public and private sectors to enter increasingly large and complex contracts for the supply of goods and services.

Putting a real-life perspective to this complexity, one of the top 10 construction projects of the 20th century was the Hoover Dam, in Nevada. The contract for the Hoover Dam was 172 pages long (100 pages of text, and 72 drawings). There were 8 defined terms in the contract.

By the late 20th century, and into the 21st century, deal-closers developed their 'art' to the point where a PPP contract suite for building a school, hospital, road, etc., is 13,500 pages long, with 5,000 defined terms (referenced 100,000 times through the contracts), and with 16,000 clause-clause or other cross references. This is what the deal-closers and their legal advisers pass over to the contract management team to manage for up to 50+ years. After his deal-close euphoria subsided, the project director on the largest PPP project in the UK referred to the sheer complexity of the contracts for the project as being an "unintended tidal wave of risk", which required prompt management to bring under control.

It is in this context that it must be recognised that, while human resources are core to the success of complex contracts, they actually comprise just one part of the formula for successful projects:

(People ▼) + (Best Tools & Processes ▲) = Successful Projects

A simple truth is that most projects cannot have the very best skilled or experienced people in each role; either because they are not available or the project is unable to afford them (a reality that has become starker with the ever growing pressures on organisations to "do more with less"). And the problem is exacerbated by the fact that people move on. When they do, their knowledge and experience is largely lost on the project they were engaged on; let alone captured and shared for the benefit of other projects within an organisation's portfolio. Given the inevitability of these people issues, it is common sense to invest in best tools and processes to ensure a detailed understanding of the contracts, as well as to capture & share knowledge, and manage risk & compliance.

As in all walks of life, technology is rapidly evolving to meet the people and complexity challenges referred to above. In relation to the engineering, design, construction and asset management aspects of projects, Building Information Management **('BIM')** software is now seen as an essential part of the future. In the U.K. the 'Government Construction Strategy', published by the Cabinet office on 31 May 2011, states the Government's intention to require collaborative 3D BIM (with all project and asset information, documentation and data being electronic) on all its projects by 2016. Even now, however, 3D BIM is rapidly being overtaken by nD BIM (augmenting the three primary spatial dimensions (width, height and depth) with time as the fourth dimension (4D) and cost as the fifth (5D), etc.).

In the same way as BIM was developed for drawings, equipment and space, the Intelligent Document Format **('IDF')** has been developed for textual documents such as complex contracts, guidelines, regulations, reports, etc. IDF is a very powerful use of HTML and associated technologies.

A little bit more history. Again, going back to the 20th century, MS Word was released 30+ years ago by Microsoft for the purpose of authoring and editing documents. It is fit for that purpose. Still in the 20th century, 20+ years ago, PDF was released by Adobe for the purpose of sealing and printing documents. It is fit for that purpose. Both these formats are 2D. Both were developed pre-Web. Neither of these 2D formats are fit for the purpose of understanding complex contracts and associated knowledge and business processes.

IDF is currently 5D, but will soon evolve to 6D - predictive. The dimensions of IDF are:

IDF Dimension	Description
3D	The 3D component of IDF is depth of document reading and understanding. IDF provides web-based 3D navigation of documents on PCs, tablets and mobile with: (i) All defined terms being pulled up as pop-ups at the click of a mouse wherever they are referred to, no matter whether they come from the agreement in question, or from another document; (ii) 100% pin-point hyperlinking of all clause-to-clause references or other linkages within and between documents; (iii) Interactive, full-text, relational database searching within and across projects; (iv) Contract management guidance from the contract management manual linked directly from the relevant clauses; and (v) Seamless integration with business / social media applications such as Yammer, Lync, SharePoint News, Huddle, etc.
4D	The 4D component of IDF is time. Documents and associated knowledge and business process evolve and change over time. IDF is a dynamic format. IDF interactive clauses push information, knowledge and tasks to relevant users as and when they need it. The clauses become an active part of project delivery: making the complex both manageable & usable: (i) The agreements are always fully up to date, with all amendments incorporated, but with an icon linking to the amendment history of any paragraph. Timeline sliders will allow you to slide your contract back through its history. (ii) Any relevant knowledge is pushed to a user as they view a clause (whether it be minutes of a meeting as to how the parties agreed the clause is to operate in practice, a legal opinion, technical report, flow chart, etc) (iii) Tasks / obligations which need to be performed are attached directly at the relevant clause, with "Just-in-Time" reminders being automatically sent to the relevant person direct from the clause. A full audit of the task performance, along with verification and compliance evidence, is captured behind the clause as the steps of task completion take place.
5D	The 5D component of IDF is cost. Costs can be attached to the relevant clause or issue
6D	The 6D component of IDF will be predictive. There are exciting opportunities arising from this; some quicker to achieve than others. Examples include: (i) Hot spot detection and heat mapping, with alerts sent for the contractual issues which are looked at currently and over time across portfolios of projects, giving early warning as to potential issues and or areas in which training may assist. (ii) Extracting information from data sets such as expected or actual rainfalls and plugging into project management software (eg. Prima Vera), and connecting with contractual notice clauses such as delays for inclement weather. (iii) Detecting trends or patterns in changing risk allocation in project, construction or finance documents on new projects.

While the benefits of IDF are self-evident for any high-value documents, the particular value of IDF for projects can be looked at in the context of the recent British Standard - BS 11000: Collaborative Business Relationships. The standard is in the process of being adapted as an International Standard (ISO 27001). BS 11000 certification is now rapidly being sought or required on major projects in the UK. It utilises an eight phase model, from project concept through to disengagement; covering the people, tools and processes elements of the formula for successful projects.

Certification requires the project to focus on, amongst other things: relationship management; effective sharing of knowledge; innovation and management systems & processes.

Before Intelligent Documents, parties to a contract generally managed them in silos: each party having its own version of the contract with all its amendments; its own table of contractual obligations; its own contract management manual (at least in theory, if not in practice!); etc.

BS 11000 has increased industry recognition that the contract is the glue which is binding the parties together to deliver agreed objectives for agreed rewards, and that a silo mentality to the management of the contract is inefficient, risky and harmful to establishing the best relationships.

With IDF and a focus on the people collaborating effectively in projects, best practice is now as follows:

- All parties have online access to the same fully up-to-date version of the contract in IDF.
- For Government contracts, the public has access to an online redacted version of the contract in IDF. This is 5* transparency, according to the rating system of Professor Sir Tim Berners-Lee, the founder of the world-wide-web.
- When the parties agree how a clause is to be interpreted in practice, that agreement is captured and shared at the clause for the benefit of new staff, advisers, etc. The same applies for knowledge within an organisation; turning personal knowledge into corporate knowledge.

- There is a single, common contract management manual or guide that the parties have agreed between them for the management of the project; again embedded at each relevant clause of the contract for quick reference. In the new PF2 model contracts in the UK, the Government mandates that the contractors are to provide this manual. This is due to a lack of available resources within Government.
- The parties agree a common contractual matrix of obligations: who has to do what, by when, and it what circumstances. "Just-in-Time" reminders of these obligations are sent to the responsible user direct from the relevant clause. Once the obligation is completed by the relevant person, an automated email goes to the verifier from the other party for confirmation that the obligation is satisfactorily performed. The compliance information now sits behind the clause, along with a complete audit trail of its completion.
- Using social media tools, team discussions can be integrated seamlessly with the relevant technical or contract clauses.
- For organisations with portfolios of projects, the collation of a library containing all projects instantly provides an extremely powerful knowledge hub for the organisation.

Picking up on a number of Charles' key themes:

1. Project results can be safeguarded by combining technical processes with excellence of the human inputs at all levels

2. One of the keys to eliminating risk is to have an automated system for generating/reminding people of tasks that are due or close to due, to ensure that contract obligations are met on time and not overlooked.

3. The parties need to know and be educated on the contract documents inside out and backwards, which is not easy; and understand the obligations and risk transfers contained within them.

Making contract documents intelligent is a quick, easy and extremely powerful solution for achieving each of the above.

And to conclude with my own mantra for excellence in project and contract management; which necessitates ensuring that competent people and the best tools and processes are seamlessly integrated at the outset of a project:

Do it once: do it right!

Biography – Graham Thomson

Graham Thomson has 40 years' experience in construction and major projects globally. Prior to co-founding Affinitext, Graham had an international reputation for facilitating resolution of complex legal and commercial disputes as a partner with Mallesons Stephen Jaques, based in Hong Kong, and previously with Masons, based in the UK.

Before embarking on his legal career, Graham qualified as an engineer and spent 10 years in large scale international project management.

This unique combination of international project management and legal experience led Graham to develop a keen interest in the use of leading information technology to enable efficient and successful execution of major projects.

Co-founding Affinitext was a natural progression of his experience and interest and, with exponential adoption, Affinitext is currently used on over $300 billion of projects world-wide.

www.affinitext.com

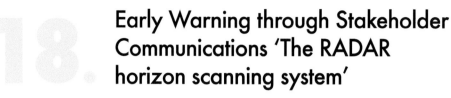

Early Warning through Stakeholder Communications 'The RADAR horizon scanning system'

By Edward Moore, BSc LLB(Hons)
Chief Executive ResoLex UK

Projects can be meticulously planned to the highest degree of technical detail, use the highest quality materials, the latest construction processes and techniques but they always have the unknown element....people.

Michael Dell has been quoted explaining his vision of the future *"The factory of the future will have two employees. A man and a dog. The man is there to feed the dog and the dog is there to stop the man touching the machines!"*

In the construction industry we do not have the luxury of an ever increasing mechanised process; in fact the contrary is true. As the size and complexity of projects grow, so does the size and complexity of the delivery teams.

It is in this highly fluid area of interpersonal dynamics that stakeholder engagement and communications is essential and where investment in the monitoring and management of inter-personal and inter-team dynamics pays large dividends.

This chapter will explore best practice in stakeholder engagement and communication and their close link with effective project risk management.

What is coming over the horizon on your project?

Governments and organisations, at a corporate level, use horizon scanning to assess threats and mitigate risk. So it is not a huge leap to see the value in applying the same principles to projects. The challenge is to find out those events that might influence, positively or negatively, the successful outcome of a project. As with governmental or corporate horizon scanning the aim is to discover what it is that you do not know about your project.

The place to start looking when trying to understand the human dynamics of a project and identifying what may be coming over the horizon is amongst the stakeholders.

When referring to stakeholders this is not jargon for the delivery team but refers to all the different people and groups of people who have a stake in the outcome of the project. If engaged in the right way these groups will provide all the information needed to ensure that the project is delivered successfully as they have the insight and information to feedback on everything from the business case through delivery risk to handover.

Herein lies the challenge! How to effectively and practically engage with a disparate group of stakeholders?

Effective stakeholder engagement requires effective stakeholder communications and effective communications requires completing a feedback loop with stakeholders, not just an information broadcast.

The initial basis of most relationships is reciprocity and this is the same for project stakeholders. Personal engagement will not be achieved by either just requesting feedback or just providing information. The projects we have seen achieve the most successful engagement of stakeholders are those that regularly deliver information and allow individuals to comment back on project concerns, successes or any topics of personal importance.

In addition to generating better engagement, feedback plays an important role in understanding the effectiveness of the stakeholder and project communications and the working dynamics of the stakeholder base and delivery team. The feedback opportunity with the stakeholder base is not reserved for testing technical data but offers the important added potential to understand individual perceptions of the project and the information the participants are receiving about it.

Understanding the stakeholder's perceptions enables the management of a project to understand and manage risk at a level seldom achieved using traditional processes.

Everyone processes information differently. Perspectives on any issues will be determined by the individual's own personal window on the world. When a situation arises on a project each person acts on the information that they receive and responds in their own unique way based on their preconceptions, perceptions and emotions. Their resulting behaviours can be positive or detrimental to the progress of the project, but are rarely considered as risks in themselves. We believe that they are a risk and therefore can, and should, be monitored and managed.

A good example of a project benefiting from this approach is the Exemplary Low Carbon Project at the University of East Anglia (UEA).

This project was a European Bank for Regional Development (EBRD) funded project and as well as providing a teaching and business incubator building for the use of the University it also provided a project where innovative processes and materials could be used as an exemplar in the modern low carbon built environment.

Having decided to use collaborative working as the model for delivery the UEA also embraced the principles of a neutral monitoring role on their project. The first step was to establish what exactly they could monitor. A workshop was held with the project stakeholders which allowed them to explore *"what success would look like"* for all different parts of the delivery team. Once this was established and agreed by all the different composite parts of the team it was possible to build a delivery plan that would allow each project team member to achieve their personal and corporate goals whilst contributing to overall project success.

Once established, this *"Modus Operandi"* for the project was turned into a project charter for all stakeholders to physically sign up to. What this also gave was the blueprint for establishing what behaviours would be needed for the charter to really work and therefore what needed to be monitored on the project.

The areas identified were:

- Whether the perceived final outcome of the project (at the time of asking) would achieve or exceed stakeholder expectations for the project?
- Was the project progressing in a way that would deliver the project aspirations?
- Was communication conducted in an open and honest manner?
- Were individual contributions communicated to and listened to by the senior management team (SMT)?
- Were the innovative elements of the project (processes and materials) capable of being commercially replicated on other projects?
- What was the level of collaboration between team members?
- Was the delivery team proactively identifying and mitigating risks?

The project team agreed that if all of these were being answered positively then the project would deliver successfully across the board.

In addition to these project wide behavioural elements, and in fact in helping to achieve the last one, the project stakeholders would also be asked to evaluate the top risks on the risk register and be able to identify other issues or risks they believed were not being addressed anywhere else.

The Project team used the ResoLex RADAR system (http://www.resolex.com) as a communication portal to deliver monthly project news to the extended stakeholder base and complete the communication loop by asking for feedback on the areas mentioned above and on the technical risks from the risk register.

The results of the monthly project evaluation exercises were analysed by a panel of industry experts who created a report which was delivered back to the project stakeholders.

The result of this process meant that each monthly meeting of the SMT had a report which formed part of the agenda and identified how all the project stakeholders perceived the project was delivering against the desired objectives and behaviours, as set out in the charter, and what, if any, risks they were concerned about.

"Our project is a cutting edge exemplar project in both form and approach and in keeping with this we embraced an innovative approach to communication. We find that the RADAR report provided us with real insight into our scheme, just as we hoped. We felt that we might miss this information through only using traditional methods. The reports have added value by enabling us to tackle issues early, reducing conflict and ultimately helping save time and money."
John French, Project Director, University of East Anglia

The benefits to the project identified by the project director above gave the project the feedback loop needed to generate engagement with the project stakeholders. The additional feedback gave clarity to the risk management process and confidence that not only were traditional technical risks being identified and mitigated but that the project had a handle on the human dynamics of the project and the risks associated with them.

The premise of the monitoring and management mentioned in the case study above is that the information and knowledge that the project needs to achieve for successful project delivery is contained within the delivery team, but the challenge is gaining access to it, understanding it in the context of the project and ensuring that the ever-limited resources are deployed on the right issue at the right time.

The two key areas to identify are:

1. Specific risks which are either new to the project or the delivery team feel are not currently being managed or mitigated effectively;

2. The divergence of perceptions between the delivery teams about a known risk or the general project progress.

Horizon scanning for new risks or ineffective management or mitigation enables this information to be communicated across the project delivery team so that all parties are aware of the risks and their role in managing or mitigating them. The elimination of surprise provides for a clearer and more strategic approach to risk on the project.

The divergence of perceptions between teams is a more difficult risk to quantify; after all it is just personal opinion, some of them may in fact be wrong, so why go to the bother of understanding it?

As I touched on earlier in this chapter, it is an individual's perception, or opinion, that drives their behaviour on the project. Therefore if key individuals or different members of the delivery team have diverging opinions about issue X they are unlikely to have a coherent approach to resolving or managing it. From our experience, this is the seed of a dispute.

All of us working in construction are acutely aware of the moment on a project where a manageable issue turns into a dispute. The red mist descends, personal and professional egos stand between swift consensual resolution and full blown dispute. There is, however, a time of opportunity when a growing issue can be worked through without substantially affecting the project; provided that the issue is identified and dealt with early. It is at this moment where the delivery of professional dispute services offer almost incalculable value to clients and the issue can be resolved in tandem with the progression of the project.

When articulating the value of effective horizon scanning on a project it is important to consider the real cost of escalating disputes. It is unlike insurance which, until something goes wrong, is just a cost. By taking the results of a horizon scanning exercise and effectively communicating them across the project delivery team you can increase engagement and actually decrease the likelihood of issues escalating into disputes or unmanaged risks damaging the project. The transparency of information and knowledge on the project also enables the ever-limited project resources to be effectively targeted at areas of the project most in need at the most appropriate time.

Biography – Edward Moore

Edward has been Chief Executive at ResoLex since 2004, during this time he has worked with some of the country's leading project risk experts on creating RADAR, a web based project horizon scanning and risk monitoring tool. The service has been developed to understand the human dynamics of risk management that bridges the gap between forensic data and the perceptions of project stakeholders which often leads to breakdown in communications and increased risk. Under the RADAR banner Edward is currently working with Higher Education, Housing and Infrastructure clients as part of the Risk Management process on projects.

Outside of his commercial work, Edward is Chairman of Concordis International, an international peace building charity working in conflict areas using mediation to build dialogue and relationships of mutual trust to develop and implement policies that improve human security and lay firm foundations for lasting peace.

www.resolex.com

Risk Management and the Relation to Success — in the North American Context

By John McArthur Dip. Env Pl, BLA
President, Kiewit Development Company, Omaha, Nebraska, USA

My recent background has focused on Public Private Partnerships so my comments and views come from this perspective. Additionally, the comments and approaches that follow are based on the premise that securing the project is a result of a highly competitive process. I have held senior positions in engineering firms and construction companies and for the past 11 years, I have established North American businesses for two different infrastructure investor/constructors. During this period, I have bid over 30 P3 projects and had success in nine, totalling a capital value of USD$8B. Both wins and losses lead to a vast library of lessons learned giving invaluable insights into the process of Risk Management.

Risk Management is a process not a single activity or event. Avoiding the identification of risks, resulting in lack of their effective management, is the most common cause of projects not being fully successful, or failing completely. The process involves looking back, analyzing historical information, drawing conclusions from this process and then putting into place measures embodied in the process of Risk Management. Conclusions drawn from an open and objective review of past projects, both the successful and unsuccessful ones, will provide the ingredients for a Risk Management process. It is often best to involve senior management that was not involved in the past projects being reviewed. It is difficult to provide objective critical analysis of projects that one has been directly involved in managing. Team members that have been part of an unsuccessful project in the past have difficulty seeing what went wrong – they can't see the forest for the trees.

Successful Risk Management comes down to the human factor. Regardless of how detailed the plans for managing risk, or how integrated into the design and construction process they are, effectively managing the people that are required to deploy these plans will determine ultimate success. This means understanding the various personality types involved in a project and using the best management methods to bring out the optimum performance in people. This must of course be done in the context of a comprehensive Project Management Plan.

Risk Management in North American projects is generally similar to other parts of the world. Probably the key difference in the United States results from there being a history of litigation arising from construction issues. There is a general propensity to take legal action to compensate wronged (or believed to be wronged) parties. For this reason, many larger construction companies have significant internal legal departments and equally sizeable in-house insurance and risk management teams. With possible litigation looming, in-house insurance and risk management teams have developed sophisticated risk analysis processes. As a result, they have considerable involvement in initial and ongoing project decision making.

It is common for the parties to end up in lengthy court battles in situations where disputes cannot be resolved by Dispute Resolution Boards (DRB's). This can be avoided by placing significant emphasis on establishing good client relationships prior to the bidding cycle which subsequently continue throughout the construction process.

Relationship of Success to Risk Management

Success derives from well-planned and executed *Risk Management.*

Golden Ears Bridge, Vancouver, under construction

Determining *Success* can only derive from a common definition of the term.

What are the definitions of Risk (management) and Success? Using Wikipedia and Webster's Dictionary, as the sources, they are:

'**Risk management** is the identification, assessment, and prioritization of risks (defined in ISO 31000 as the effect of uncertainty on objectives) followed by coordinated and economical application of resources to minimize, monitor and control the probability and/or impact of unfortunate events...'

Wikipedia defines **Success** as:

'The achievement of a **goal** – the opposite of failure'

Webster's Dictionary defines it as:

'The correct or **desired result** of an attempt'

With success as a goal, applying Risk Management as defined above, will lead to successful projects.

When a project is about to begin, whether a P3 or a Design/Build delivery model, there is a sequence of activities that must occur in order to increase the likelihood of successful delivery, which are:

1. If one doesn't exist, establish a Risk Management Matrix (simplified example follows);

2. Review lessons learned from past similar projects – apply them;

3. Select the best team suited to the type of project being delivered (designers, advisors, core team members and project managers);

4. Know the client – ideally from past experience – adjust approach to suit;

5. Establish a regular team member communication protocol and follow it;

6. Establish a single point of contact with the client in order to maintain clear communication;

7. Establish a Project Management Plan (PMP) – that entails setting out roles and responsibilities, team organization and reporting relationships with communication to all team members getting full team 'buy-in' and acceptance;

8. Establish clear leadership and control of the team reflecting it in the PMP;

9. Begin work!

Interesting to note that items 1-8 are undertaken before any project specific construction work has begun. Building the proper foundation is no less important figuratively than it is literally in creating a physical building foundation, or sub-structure.

Well-managed project risks lead to project success. The process begins with identifying categories of risk and planning for methods of dealing with these risks. In general terms, once risks are identified, methods of dealing with them need to be put into place. If risks are not identified and managed they could potentially lead to any combination of the following:

1. Project schedule not being met – potential for liquidated damages being applied;

2. Project being over budget – for fixed price contracts the contractor generally absorbs the overrun where there are no remedies for compensation;

3. Termination by the owner for a contractor default – failure to perform the work as specified;

4. Liability for third party damages – subcontractors, third parties;

5. Liens being placed against the work;

6. Counterparty law-suits for damages;

Following is a list of some of these key risk management methods:

1. Schedule planning and management – ensuring enough schedule float has been provided – scheduling to accommodate unknown permitting time frames;

2. Insurance – certain risks can be insured against – business interruption liability with defined caps in exposure;

3. Specification review – prior to contract award, plan to review and revise specifications with owner to ensure a deliverable project;

4. Personnel – assigning the correct number, experience level and organization structure to successfully manage the project – for example in urban areas, assigning a single person or team to deal with utilities locates and relocates;

5. Contract with owner – when the opportunity exists prior to contract award, review unfavourable or poor value for money (for the owner) contract terms in an attempt to correct.

There are at least four categories within which projects can measure success and therefore risks can be managed successfully. There are varying degrees of success derived from risk management, but ultimately a highly successful project achieves all project goals. In order to establish a framework for showing how to achieve success, it is worth reviewing at least four key areas. Achieving goals and successful risk management can be expressed in the following categories:

1. A project with a safe work record;

2. A project that has achieved all of its financial targets;

3. A project that has fostered and maintained personal and corporate relationships;

4. A project that has met or exceeded its technical requirements.

The four categories within which to measure success and to employ risk management methods are therefore:

1. Safety
    a. All stakeholders buying into and following safety protocols;
    b. No recordable incidents;
    c. All participants empowered to work safe (prime and subcontractors, owners, consultants etc.).

2. Finance or Economics
    a. 'On time' and on budget' delivery;
    b. Acceptable ROI for all participants;
    c. Minimal Claims;
    d. Subcontractors and suppliers ROI achieved.

3. Relationships
    a. Happy client;
    b. Dispute resolution managed fairly and properly;
    c. Good on-going relationships with various approving and permitting authorities;
    d. Happy partners, designers and internal team members.

4. Technical
    a. Clients (users) program requirements met;
    b. Benchmark technical specifications met or exceeded;
    c. Efficient and economical design.

Risk Management techniques should be designed and used to ensure success in the above four areas.

These are the key measures of success, but how do you go about the process of winning the project and delivering success? What process do you need to follow in order to be able to undertake a project that can then be measured as successful or not?

Planning for Success and Managing Risks

Success is not the result of luck. It is the result of careful planning. *'Plan the work'* and *'work to plan'* are keys to success and the fundamental basis for risk management. A famous golfer once said that *'the more I practice, the luckier I get'*. The same idiom applies although the 'practice' component in the context of a construction project would be preparation and planning. I believe that 50% of the contribution to the success of a project occurs before anyone actually gets on a construction site. The same level of effort should be expended in selecting projects as in building them.

There are several key planning activities that should be used in preparation for creating a successful project. These activities should take the form of a Risk Mitigation Matrix where possible. Filling out the Risk Matrix should then be one of the evaluation tools used in deciding whether or not to pursue a project. Keeping in mind the categories for success measurement, the planning activities (or risk measuring categories) are as follows:

Go/No-Go Stage (Bid stage)

1. Project Type
    a. Do we have experience with this type of project – have we successfully constructed this project type in the past?
    b. Are there particular technical issues with the project type and do we know what they are and how to mitigate them?
    c. Do we have a partner(s) that do have the specific experience required, with corporate philosophies aligned?

2. Personnel
    a. Do we have personnel with specific successful experience in the project type?
    b. Can we commit senior project personnel to the project for the project duration?
    c. Do we know the sub-trades and have relationships with them in the local area?

3. Processes and Procedures
    a. Do we have proper internal and external communications skills and procedures in place and known to all parties?
    b. Do we prepare and follow a comprehensive Project Management Plan (PMP) and do we communicate this to all team members including the client?
    c. Do we have internal safety committees and clearly defined work procedures and processes?
    d. Do we provide the proper safety training both on and off site?

Golden Ears Bridge, Vancouver, under construction

4. Authorities and Local Conditions
   a. Do we have experience dealing with local authorities and permitting agencies (building, utilities, planning, traffic, rail, etc.)
   b. Do we fully understand local approval processes and timetables?
   c. Do we fully understand the selection process – (lowest price, best value, highest technical score)?

5. Technical
   a. Are the consultants the best for the project at hand?
   b. Have we worked with them in the past?
   c. Do we fully understand all liabilities and is insurance available for the same?

6. Competition
   a. Do we know the competition?
   b. What is their financial strength?
   c. Do they have bonding capacity?
   d. Who are their advisors?
   e. What is their track record with the client?

In designing the Matrix, key evaluation criteria leading to a 'go or no go' decision should occupy the vertical axis. The horizontal axis should contain qualitative categories and mitigation actions that when filled in properly, will result in a risk management plan. In fact, a project will ideally have multiple levels of Risk Matrix, beginning with a 'go/no go' analysis or matrix. Beyond this category, matrices can be prepared for all aspects of the project as follows:

1. Specifications
   a. General conditions;
   b. Division content – vague or clearly defined;
   c. Contradictions between sections;
   d. Technically correct.

2. Drawings
   a. Clear and complete;
   b. Drawing and section references – complete and accurate;
   c. Explanatory;
   d. Technically correct.

3. Project Mobilization
   a. Site access;
   b. Permits;
   c. Equipment availability;
   d. Long delivery item ordering and costing.

4. Consultants
   a. Experience;
   b. Integrated into the construction team;
   c. Previous experience working together.

Following is an example of some of the components of an initial 'go/no go' risk matrix.

Risk Management Matrix	'Go/No-go' stage						
Category	Potential Risk	Experience Level	Technical Issues	Available Partners & Staff	Safety Record on Similar	Do we know the Authorities?	Who are the competitors?
Project Type							
Personnel							
Process & Procedures							
Authorities							
Technical							
Competition							

The above table is a very generic version of a matrix that would contain many more categories and be significantly more comprehensive at the 'go/no go' stage of the risk mitigation process.

Following is a generic risk matrix based on the assumption the project is proceeding. Once again, it is a summarized version of what would likely be multiple matrices that would relate more specifically to various components of the project.

Risk Management Matrix							
Category	Potential Risk	Schedule Mitigation	Price	Insure	Push Back to Client	Combination of measures - other	Risk not acceptable – do not proceed
Specifications	General						
	Conditions vague						
	Section Contradictions						
Drawings	Alternates acceptable						
Mobilization	Granular location						
	Job site lease						
	Permitting Process						

	Long Delivery Items					
Consultants	Fee Approach					

Keep in mind that when you Google 'Risk Management in Construction' you get over 64 million results. Many lengthy books have been written on the subject, so what is contained herein is only meant to point out some of the key components of Risk Management and to give brief guidance and direction as one investigates further the process of Risk Management.

Summary

The following summarizes the key components of Success through Risk Management in North American projects:

1. Success is achieved through detailed Risk Management;

2. Risk management Matrices should be used as follows:
   a. Initial Go, No-Go decision making
   b. Bidding Phase;
   c. Construction Phase;
   d. Post Construction – Warranty phase.

3. Risk Management Plans should form an integral part of a detailed Project Management Plan;

4. The Plan and the Risk Management process should be explained and understood by all team members including the client;

5. Rapid and effective communication of issues throughout the construction cycle (design through post construction) is critical to managing and mitigating risks;

6. Effective analysis of the mitigation measures to be employed should take into account the potential additional cost that could be simply applied, versus other less costly (but effective) approaches;

7. Every person involved in a project has a responsibility to identify, communicate and manage risks in the same way they should be empowered to do the same related to safety matters.

8. **Regardless of the level of technical sophistication built in to risk analysis, the process is applied by humans. Making sure that project participants are *'invested'* in delivering its success will reduce risks, or ensure they are mitigated. Often, a portion of team member remuneration tied to successful risk mitigation can be effective;**

9. Another effective method of managing risk derives from a pre-construction partnering session, followed by at least annual sessions during the course of construction. Again, this approach focuses on the interpersonal relationships of 'partners' (client and design build team) establishing direct lines of communication and a hierarchy of issue resolution based on each party's project objectives.

Biography – John McArthur

John McArthur has over 35 years' experience in the design, construction and infrastructure investment business throughout North America. His education in urban planning and landscape architecture comprised his formal educational training and that coupled with his extensive experience forms the basis of his understanding of Risk Management. During his career he has developed projects with one of Canada's largest real estate development companies through-out Canada. He also spent several years with a major Canadian construction company working on a variety of large building projects. Since 2003 he has been in the Public Private Partnership investment business, initially for an international German construction/investment company and more recently with a large American construction/investment company. Over the course of a long career he has seen Risk Management develop to become the sophisticated process that it is today. Risk Management is now widely employed by designers, subcontractors, owners, investors, rating agencies, insurance/bonding companies and public agencies. He notes that in the past it was only given a minor level of recognition, but now it has become one of the trademarks of not only top tier companies, but also is a process utilized by most that are involved both directly and indirectly, in the construction business.

Corporate Governance and Effective Operational Risk Management

Stringent corporate governance should be fundamental to any corporate management process, and we suggest the following items be closely considered.

An *"anticipatory"* process should be used to alert the senior management team at the first indication of a possible risk, so that preventative or mitigating measures can be put in place. This process should be applied at all stages of a project - from the initial concept, through the tender stage, D&C and during operations.

REPORTING REQUIREMENTS AND PROCEDURES TO CONTROL AND CONTAIN POTENTIAL RISKS

Project Risk Schedules

From the outset, with projects of all sizes, it is important to identify and schedule all potential risks. This should be a key element in undertaking project feasibilities and planning and in preparing Bids. The various risks can be weighted for probability and harmful value and if considered necessary contingency allowances can be included in the cost build-ups. Remember of course that all potential risks are unlikely to happen on one project, so making a cost contingency for all of them is likely to make the feasibility unrealistic and not viable or make the Bid uncompetitive.

There are plenty of typical risk schedules and software programs available that include probability and cost contingency weighting. We have not included samples because this book is not meant to be an operations manual; it is sufficient that we cover the principles and importance of having a robust risk management process.

However, we have included an org chart at the end of this chapter that shows how to structure the process for a major project, with section leaders reporting to a dedicated risk manager.

Risk Management and Key Issues Reports should be produced monthly or more frequently if required, for all ongoing projects. Risk Management Reports should be designed as check-lists to assist managers, but experience in recognising situations at an early stage and common sense in addressing them are fundamental. Managers should be required to report all potential risks to the investments.

The key requirement is to identify potential risks at the earliest possible time so that they can be either dealt with promptly and eliminated as a risk or mitigated to the maximum extent possible. This requires an acceptance of the principle by site managers and those to whom they report and this can be more difficult to achieve than you would imagine.

The reason this is difficult is of course human nature. Often managers will take the view that they will solve the problem quickly so they don't have to alert the potential risk to those higher up. They seem to think, quite wrongly, that the early identification and reporting of a potential risk is a reflection on their capability personally and their sense of propriety is offended, so they keep the problem to themselves and try to resolve it before the next monthly risk management report – a big mistake! They overlook or do not understand that once they report the issue they are making life easier for themselves by sharing it with others and that they then have the combined weight and experience of the company in there to help them sort it out. It is very common problem, a mind-set problem.

Project Executive Summary

So, the question *is 'On a major project, how can senior management be sure that the site team is being really diligent and efficient in their overall management; that they are reporting things factually and accurately; and that they will comply with the principle of 'early warning' risk management?'*

There are two processes that can be adopted that should enable senior management to be able to sleep at night.

Early Warning *'by exception'* reporting for the risk management control of multiple projects

All construction companies have standardized reporting and control formats for their projects - financial, operational, program, quality assurance, health and safety, corporate governance and environmental compliance, etc.

For *'early warning'* risk management there are some simple formats that can be used on a monthly basis, but surprisingly many construction companies do not use them. These formats are based on drawing up a list of key areas to be monitored and if there is a risk issue or potential issue with any of these areas then this should be immediately notified by the project manager to the next level and also entered into the monthly report, with details. It certainly should not be left until the next monthly report for notification. There are two strong reasons for immediate notification:

- It allows the maximum amount of time to prevent or mitigate the risk as much as possible.
- The project manager will have team support to handle the issue *('two heads are better than one')*. It becomes the company's problem, not just the problem of the project manager.

The monthly *'early warning'* reports can include the following typical items for monitoring, with boxes for ticking in the affirmative, or green and orange traffic lights. The operations manager supervising the project should jointly sign-off the monthly report with the project manager.

Confirm that:

▶ The direct construction costs-to-date are within budget   Y
▶ The direct construction costs-to-complete are within budget   N details attached
▶ The preliminaries and overheads are within budget   Y
▶ The design consultants' costs are within budget   Y
▶ Progress-to-date is in line with the program   Y
▶ Progress claims and payments are in line with the program   Y
▶ The Quality Assurance has received all third party sign-offs to date
     - Lender's technical advisor   Y
     - Client's technical adviser   Y
     - Design consultants   Y
▶ All required statutory approvals have been received   N details attached
▶ All insurance policies are in place and premiums paid   Y
▶ All Health and Safety requirements are being met   Y
▶ All Environmental compliance matters are in order   N details attached
▶ All corporate governance items and statutory accounts are
up-to-date (refer to the check-list)   N details attached
▶ All contract documentation processing is up-to-date and not
outstanding more than 10 working days   Y
▶ Confirm that there are no detrimental contractor or subcontractor
human resource issues outstanding at the moment   Y
▶ Confirm that there are no detrimental communications or relationship
Issues between any of the stakeholders   Y

This executive level *'early warning'* risk management format is designed to be easy and fast to complete and thus suitable for multiple projects being run by large companies. Strong discipline is required in the preparation of the aspects such as budgets, targets, programs and protocols; and honest and accurate completion by project managers and their supervisors is essential.

Really Effective Risk Management

is all about

Having the Right People in the Right Positions

Anticipating, Anticipating, Anticipating

and being

Ahead of the Game

Independent audits

Most companies do have an internal audit process and these audits should be done on a regular basis, say quarterly, to ensure that the monthly reporting is being accurately and honestly carried out, but internal auditing does have its drawbacks and these are examined in Chapters 27 and 28.

A regular independent audit is a cost-effective way of providing back-up to the internal reporting and auditing process. Unfortunately it is sometimes hard to convince the senior management of many construction companies that this is a prudent method of risk management; that is until they suffer a big loss on a project that could have been prevented had it been picked up earlier.

Corporate Compliance & Obligations Diary – with every project there are a significant number of reporting and compliance obligations that should be undertaken on a regular basis and it is useful to have an annual Compliance & Obligations Diary to ensure that the necessary work is prepared in advance and deadlines are not missed. The Diary can include all matters and reports pertaining to the following corporate responsibilities:

- External stakeholders
- Statutory returns
- Annual accounts, audits and tax returns
- Insurance premium renewals
- Securities institutes
- Licensing
- Local Government
- Health & Safety
- Environmental
- Training and Apprenticeship Schemes

Insurances Register – a Register should be maintained that includes the Policy details and Premium renewal dates of all insurances relating to the Group and the relevant projects, Clients, Third Parties (Authorities, Subcontractors, etc.).

BID RISK MANAGEMENT - TEAM STRUCTURE

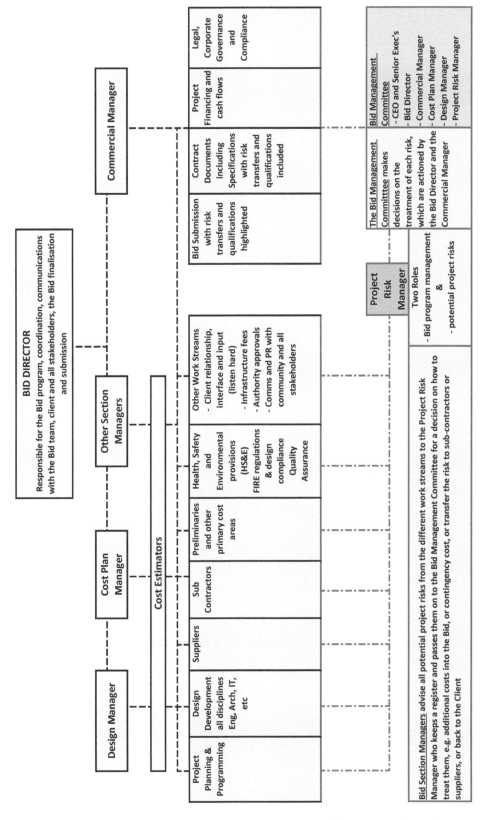

BID DIRECTOR

Responsible for the Bid program, coordination, communications with the Bid team, client and all stakeholders, the Bid finalisation and submission

Design Manager | Cost Plan Manager | Other Section Managers | Commercial Manager

Cost Estimators

| Project Planning & Programming | Design Development all disciplines Eng, Arch, IT, etc | Suppliers | Sub Contractors | Preliminaries and other primary cost areas | Health, Safety and Environmental provisions (HS&E) FIRE regulations & design compliance Quality Assurance | Other Work Streams - Client relationship, interface and input (listen hard) - Infrastructure fees - Authority approvals - Comms and PR with community and all stakeholders |

| Bid Submission with risk transfers and qualifications highlighted | Contract Documents including Specifications with risk transfers and qualifications included | Project Financing and cash flows | Legal, Corporate Governance and Compliance |

Project Risk Manager

Two Roles
- Bid program management
&
- potential project risks

Bid Management Committee

The Bid Management Committtee makes decisions on the treatment of each risk, which are actioned by the Bid Director and the Commercial Manager

Bid Management Committee
- CEO and Senior Exec's
- Bid Director
- Commercial Manager
- Cost Plan Manager
- Design Manager
- Project Risk Manager

Bid Section Managers advise all potential project risks from the different work streams to the Project Risk Manager who keeps a register and passes them on to the Bid Management Committee for a decision on how to treat them, e.g. additional costs into the Bid, or contingency cost, or transfer the risk to sub-contractors or suppliers, or back to the Client

Planning and Programming

Surprisingly few people are really good at planning and programming major projects. It is a very specialised skill and it is one of the most important professions in the construction and engineering industry. It is the foundation of success for all property developments, traditional construction, D&C contracts and PPPs.

The key to good planning and programming is being able to keep your eye on the bigger picture. The starting point should be the Master Plan Summary sheet and this should have no more than 20 activities on it, with its own simple Critical Path line.

No matter how big a project is, when you really examine the bigger picture there will not be any more than approximately 20 main activities that are critical to the overall delivery program. They may change during the duration of the project but the main critical activities will still be small in number. This is the sort of Master Plan Summary that senior management of multi-national clients and multi-national contractors want to look at, not several pages with 500 activities.

Behind each of the main activities there may be up to another 100 activities, which can be produced on back-up sheets, again with their own critical path line.

A common mistake made by some programmers is to produce all the activities for a project, several hundred of them, across a few A3 sheets, all beautifully in sequence and with coloured critical path lines all through them, but without a Summary sheet.

The problem with this is that:

- You can't see the big picture easily.
- The program is pretty well useless as a management tool for site section managers and trades supervisors. It is simply too much to look at every couple of days, as they should, and they will largely ignore it.
- However if you give them a concise program that only relates to their section of the work they will use it and give regular feedback to the programmer to update it. Of course they should also have a copy of the Master Plan Summary so they can see how their work fits into the bigger picture.
- With the updating, this approach is also much better than having the programmer wandering around the site coming to his own conclusions on progress without talking to the section managers and foremen, which is not uncommon but quite impractical (yes, it really happens – another breakdown in communications).

When looking at a program for a major project, with say a 3-4 year design and construction period, there are 4 things to immediately look for:

- The Master Plan Summary sheet – rarely available unless requested, but simple to do
- The date of the last revision (update)
- Anything that is really basic to the delivery process that might be missing. It happens, people get too close to the project. It might be related to design or authority approvals, construction or commissioning. In the anecdote at the end of Chapter 10 *'Project Leadership – How Bad Can It Get?'* there is a classic example of something fundamental that was missing and which had serious delay implications and should never have been missed.
- Go to the last page of the program and look at all the activities for commissioning and completion. If there is half a page of activities all bunched up into 3 or 4 months in the

bottom right hand corner then your alarm bells should start ringing, because it is a sure sign of potential trouble. This is one of the most difficult and complex periods of any large construction project, yet this bunching-up shows that the site management and the programmer have not given it much thought and invariably not enough time. This is a very common problem and is a _**high risk area.**_

The following are a few practical tips for effective planning and programming:

- The 20 activities Master Plan Summary is a _**must**_.

- Do not let the automated software do the critical path. It is clever, but it doesn't think as well as you do or know about all the implications. Think through all the issues yourself and install the critical path accordingly. There is nothing wrong with using software like MS Project, in fact you definitely should, but you must control the programming and not have the software controlling the outcome. And yes, it is not unusual to hear someone say _'that's how it came out of MS Project',_ which also shows up their inexperience.

- To get the right picture, try sitting back with your eyes shut and walk through the project in your mind and keep asking _'what has to happen to make this happen?'_ and _'what if it doesn't happen?'_

- Some of the best programmers in the world print out the A3 sheets and then attack them with their big red pencil and ruler.

- There is quite a bit of misconception about what a critical path really is. People tend to forget that a good contractor should be flexible in organising the works around unforeseen delays in say material and equipment deliveries and has an obligation to try and mitigate overall delay, for the sake of their own pocket as much as anything. This issue of misunderstanding commonly pops up in claims for Extensions of Time. It is a complex contractual area and is a study on its own.

- Programs are sometimes designed to influence clients and lenders because of the cash flow implications (or pull the wool over their eyes with downright dishonesty). Keep well away from this practice.

- Another dangerous but not uncommon practice is 'head-in-the-sand' syndrome, where project managers have got themselves into a corner and can no longer accept reality and produce programs to protect or project the reports they are submitting.

S-Curves and their significance

S-Curves basically reflect common sense. The more effort you put into the planning and the preparation of the specifications and contractual documents up-front then the smoother will be your design and construction program; and with minimal issues, variation claims, delays and cost problems. This applies to both, clients and contractors.

S-Curves therefore are the very antithesis of so-called 'fast track' programs, which in essence say _'let's start building tomorrow and we'll sort out the design and specifications as we go, on the run'._ Over the last few decades it is rare that _'fast tracking'_ has worked well on a major project, but there have been many disastrous attempts.

However, do not confuse 'fast tracking' with 'high performance' contracting, which is all about careful and detailed planning and programming, with the difference being that it is all compressed into a much faster than normal delivery period and may involve 24/7 operations; but all still in line with the principles of a sensible S-Curve. With high performance contracts there will be a real reason for doing it this way and the costs will invariably be higher, but it is done with eyes open and with the implications known in advance.

Some years ago a starch factory blew up in Australia. It was a huge dust ignition explosion and it scattered parts of the factory over a wide area and destroyed much of it. At the time it was the only starch factory in the country and the owners had a virtual monopoly in the market, however another company had announced that they intended entering the market and had commenced planning their new factory.

The owners of the factory that blew up were determined to continue supplying their customers and immediately started flying in product from one of their overseas factories, obviously at huge cost.

The re-build of the factory was project managed on a *'high performance'* basis, with the project managers and subcontractors working hand-in-glove with the owners. It was a big task. The factory covered a whole city block and was 6 to 8 levels high on average. It was in an inner city location so the façade had to be brick to comply with City Planning and there were all sorts of other inner city location implications. The company wanted the latest technology and equipment, but the waiting list in Scandinavia was six months. They paid a premium to jump the queue and chartered Jumbos to fly it to Australia.

Two months was spent on the planning, design and authority approvals, working around the clock; with the demolition and early works happening simultaneously. The main construction started at the beginning of July and the new factory was commissioned and started production at the end of February, to everyone's amazement. It was the result of very detailed planning of every aspect.

In summary, an S-Curve demonstrates that the success of the project will be in direct proportion to the amount of forward planning, but if you cut this short then the top of the curve will most likely flatten out and result in higher costs and a longer delivery time.

The importance of S-Curves to property developers and their lenders

The S-Curve progress has vital importance to property developers who are using a high proportion of financing and also with PPPs where the financing can be as high as 90% of the total capital cost.

With all commercial projects the completion date is the trigger for the operating revenue flow and any delay can have serious consequences on the return on investment, let alone the further downside if the project runs over budget. The lenders watch this like a hawk obviously, because it does not take a very large overrun in time and cost before a project can run into serious financial trouble.

The two main things to be watching are *'progress v. program'* and *'cost-to-complete v. budget'* and these two areas can be quite accurately compared to a properly prepared S-Curve. It is important not to confuse *'cost-to-date'* with *'cost-to-complete'*, because *'cost-to-date'* is only a component of *'cost-to-complete'* which must take into account all potential additional costs that will be incurred in getting to practical completion, with the cost of additional time and 'preliminaries' being just as important as the direct construction costs.

A typical S-Curve

COST

TIME

Prudent Risk Management

Closely monitor

Progress v. Program

Cost-to-Complete v. Budget

Services Contract & Operations

Completion and Commissioning

Fit-Out

Construction

Detailed Planning Period

Design Development

Finance Agreement

Project Agreement

Watch the S-Curve progress carefully. It can be critical to success

Extensions of Time (EOTs), concurrency and associated costs – this is one of the most complex areas in construction management. Claims for EOTs and costs arise in virtually all projects, certainly in all major projects, and commonly lead to disputes over how they are assessed. We will only give a brief summary of the overall picture because many books and papers have been and continue to be produced on this topic.

From a risk management point of view it is an extremely important topic in that both parties, the client and the contractor, are trying to protect themselves financially. The stakes are big and the assessments can be difficult; and the relevant terms of contract need to be clear and precise.

<u>Guiding Principles for Delay, EOTs and Cost Reimbursement</u>

- The Lump Sum price and the Completion Date are fixed in the Contract at the time of signing to protect the client and safeguard their investment against costs incurred through contractor delays and claims. Having done this it is then necessary for the client and their consultants, such as the architect and the Engineer, to undertake their administrative responsibilities and contractual obligations in a timely and efficient manner. If this is done and the contractor is late in delivery, then Liquidated Damages (LD's) and other such penalties as written into the Contract will be applied to the contractor.

- On the other hand, the contractor is protected against LD's, penalties and costs arising out of client related delays by Extensions of Time (EOTs) and related cost reimbursement. EOTs can result from any delay caused by third parties related to the client and not under the control of the contractor, such as the architect and Engineer.

- If there is *'client-caused'* delay, e.g. lack of instruction, and simultaneously a 'contractor-caused' delay covering part or all of the same time period, e.g. lack of site labour, then under established international practice, the 'client-caused' delay takes precedence over the 'contractor-caused' delay and the contractor is entitled to the EOT and costs, because otherwise the contractor is entitled to claim that the event may have eaten into his program float.

- In certain circumstances it may be reasonable to give a proportional EOT that reflects the amount of delay attributed to each party, but only in circumstances that are quite clear in measurable terms, with any doubt being in favour of the contractor.

- The Delay Event must be shown to have been on the Critical Path for an EOT to be granted. If the specific works that initiate the EOT Claim and the flow-on sequence of works could still have been done without delaying the Completion Date (which includes previously approved EOT's) then no EOT or related costs shall be applicable.

- The contractor has an obligation to mitigate delay, if at all possible, by reorganising the site activities in order to maintain the Contract program, as adjusted for any EOTs already approved. In other words, the contractor must show that the Delay Event in question did indeed cause an extension to the Completion Date and there was no way this could be avoided.

- Where several Delay Events occur, the contractor is only entitled to the net extra time required to complete the construction. This is called Concurrency and on this basis, several Delay Events may only result in one EOT being approved even though a similar amount of delay time may apply to all of them. In this situation only one lot of fixed site costs will also be approved, but specific costs related to individual Delay Events may be approved if the contractor can prove them.

- It is possible in some situations that the contractor will be granted an EOT but no costs, which will give him protection against potential LDs. This is commonly known as *'time without money'*.

Hamburg Philharmonic Hall

- The contractor must prove the specific losses claimed in relation to Delay Events and EOTs by providing in each case an itemised breakdown of costs, which shall be evaluated on a reasonable basis.

- A contractor might assert that delayed payments have caused slow progress on site or an inability to place orders for long lead-time materials and equipment, but such an assertion should be assessed by comparing payments-to-date with the value of works-to-date, including off-site orders that have been placed.

- The contractor may be entitled to separate compensation for delayed payments, such as interest or financing costs, if this is written into the Contract, but an EOT will not necessarily be appropriate unless the delay in payment is for an unreasonable amount of time and can be shown to have caused a delay to the overall program, e.g. the delayed payment caused a delay in procurement. It is quite rare, but some contracts include an automatic EOT with Costs built into the contract that comes into play if the client misses the contractual payment deadline, such as 56 days after certification by the Engineer. This is a strong incentive to the client to make the payments on time.

Hamburg Philharmonic Hall

The following extracts are taken from an article printed in the Frankfurter Allgemeine Zeitung (newspaper) on 8 Jan 2014. In reprinting these extracts the author is not confirming or verifying the accuracy of the information, other than to say that there are several websites that have information on this project that is similar, including

http://en.wikipedia.org/wiki/Elbe_Philharmonic_Hall

http://www.gramophone.co.uk/blog/the-gramophone-blog/will-hamburgs-%E2%82%AC800m-building-site-ever-actually-become-a-concert-hall

The news article quoted the following information from a two year parliamentary enquiry which produced a 724 page report:

- The foundation stone was laid in 2007 with a two year program; the anticipated completion as of January 2014 is now 2017 – an 8 year overrun. The original cost estimate was €186m and in January 2014 €860m.
- The project was badly planned and organised from the start; it was too hurried; the tender went out too early and the contract was awarded too early, before all construction requirements were defined. The inevitable result was increased costs from extremely high claims by the builder and delays in construction; and a lot of controversy.
- The then Hamburg Mayor was extremely enthusiastic about the project, but there was no effective control by the City of its project company; the original project director reported to the mayor and had huge authority but had no one controlling him.
- There was a complex 3-way relationship between the architect, the City and the Builder which caused lots of fights and blockages, including several months of stop-work.
- Initially it was advertised with supposed foreseeable costs. From the beginning the costs were too optimistic and turned out to be way too low. The main cause of cost increase was the incomplete planning when the contract was signed, despite the warning of the architects of possible later claims.
- Hochtief, the Builder, was the only remaining bidder in December 2006. As proof that the planning at that stage made it impossible to calculate a realistic price,

Strabach is quoted saying they were not able to quote because of the incomplete technical issues.
- After a change of government the City paid two hundred million for which Hochtief agreed to complete for a fixed price and after which the architects worked directly with Hochtief.
- Since then the construction and progress has gone better, but the situation is a phenomena that is common to many public big projects.

Dispute Resolution — the benefits and risks of alternative methods

If the project is a failure then it will certainly have disputes. Failure and subsequent disputes can occur in respect of cost, program, quality and function. How these disputes are then handled is of critical importance in respect of the costs of running the dispute; the executive time involved; and the ongoing relationships of the parties.

In this Chapter we will concentrate on the following aspects of dispute management, because they contain a lot of human behaviour considerations.

- Avoiding formal disputes through early communications and negotiations
- Main considerations of the parties when they end up in a formal dispute
- What do commercial clients want out of a formal dispute process?
- Working with lawyers

It is not the purpose of this book to review the mechanics and merits of the various methods of formal and alternative (ADR) dispute resolution. In fact, there are so many publications on this subject coming forward all the time that it is hard for even experienced construction industry professionals to keep up, let alone for less experienced participants to know where to start.

For readers requiring a concise and highly authoritative book on this subject, I recommend: **"Engineers' dispute resolution handbook"** by a specialist team of authors in Keating Chambers, London; Editor: Dr Robert Gaitskell, QC, BSc (Eng.); Foreword by Professor John Uff, CBE, QC, FREng; Published by Thomas Telford, first edition 2006.

This excellent book covers *Avoiding Disputes, When Disputes Arise,* and the seven methods of formal dispute resolution – *Litigation, Arbitration, Adjudication, Mediation, Expert Determination, Early Neutral Evaluation and International Dispute Resolution.*

Avoiding formal disputes through early communications and negotiations

I am a great believer in doing everything possible to negotiate settlements and this is always my prime objective, even after the disputes have become 'formal' insofar as a Notice of Arbitration or similar has been issued.

I have expanded on this approach in Chapter 26, 'Techniques for Negotiating Settlements'.

To avoid ending up in a formal dispute that goes the whole distance, communication is the key. It is not easy to get people to sit down and talk objectively once the battle lines have been drawn, but it is possible if you go about it the right way.

Human emotion is the big obstacle, so getting around that is the challenge. If the senior management of the party in dispute, be it the investor, the contractor, the subcontractor or the government department is serious about trying to resolve the dispute before it goes to court or arbitration there are a few simple techniques that are really worth trying:

- Do not leave the handling of the matter solely in the hands of the manager or project director that has been driving it since it started. That person is likely to have too much emotional baggage attached; they also might have created the problem or let it get this far unnecessarily and therefore they will have something to prove and probably be quite defensive of their 'just cause'. In other words, they will have lost their objectivity and commercial realism. Contractors by nature tend to be adversarial and use sledge-hammer tactics (not good in a PPP).

- *Talk first – write later – and talk, talk again'* – but it does not mean you are going soft all the time.
- Try an informal cup of coffee with your adversary, out of the office of course; work on the relationship if you want to have continuing business with the other party.
- Lay your cards on the table; often adversaries are fighting at cross-purposes and have got a screwed up or inaccurate view of the position of the other side and how they might be willing to compromise. There is nothing wrong with trying a 'without prejudice' discussion.
- The best way to negotiate positively is to *'know your Contract'* and stick to being objective. You can calmly try to point out to the other party that they are using a wrong interpretation of the Contract terms.
- Always keep in mind that success in resolving issues is a direct reflection of the relationships and communications between the parties.
- Stick to the principle that it should not be a dispute, only an **issue** that needs solving through sensible discussion. Mutual goodwill is enormously valuable of course. That might have evaporated by this time, but that does not rule out compromise as a pragmatic approach.
- Often there will be grey areas in contracts, or maybe even black holes, so you can point out that it is in the interest of both parties to amend the relevant terms of Contract rather than spend a fortune trying to resolve the unsolvable.
- Always remember who has the Contract with whom – client and the contractor, but not the client with the contractor's subcontractors or suppliers, or client and design consultants; likewise the contractor does not have a Contract with the design consultants if they are directly contracted with the client. This can become confusing if the design consultants are novated over to the contractor after the project has commenced, as often happens. So when considering the rights and obligations, risk transfers and claims or disputes, it is important to keep in mind which specific parties have direct Contracts with each other.
- A three-way arrangement whereby the client has a Contract with the contractor and separate Contract with the principle design consultants will only work smoothly if the communications protocol and management platform work with discipline and efficiency, otherwise history has proven many times that this arrangement can be difficult and cause lots of problems.

Main considerations of the parties when they end up in a formal dispute

When all else fails commercial managers want a dispute resolution process that:

- Is as fast as possible, without unnecessary delay
- Minimises legal fees and executive time and disruption
- Has confidentiality if possible, e.g. arbitration
- Minimises the damage to relationships; ongoing business between parties might be a very important consideration, but so is the maintenance of personal relationships, because it is a remarkably small community in most industries and businesses and people move between companies fairly regularly these days.
- At this stage everyone wants to win obviously, but realistically there are no guarantees of this in dispute resolution – so if the result goes against you then you want to be satisfied that you have had a fair and reasonable hearing and that the decision handed down is legally and contractually correct, logical and well-reasoned.

What do commercial clients want out of a formal dispute process?

This might seem like a simplistic question but it will probably help us decide which dispute resolution process is the most suitable one to use to determine a particular dispute.

The reasons that companies enter into dispute can be many and varied and they have an important bearing on how a dispute should be managed.

I categorise these reasons as being either 'tactical' or 'genuine'.

There are five reasons that I classify as being tactical:

- To enable an independent party to decide the issue, because the negotiators are not authorised or prepared to make a decision
- To encourage settlement, because the other party won't talk
- To create leverage on the other party for some related reason, financial or company political, e.g. a trade-off position
- To defend the ego or incompetence of a manager or a previous management decision
- To delay payment

Tactical reasons can be very frustrating, time consuming and expensive, but it is a fact of life and human nature that they occur and when they do, we need to be best equipped to deal with them.

However, there are also some genuine reasons why people fail to settle their differences and end up in formal proceedings and most of them will fall under one of the following two categories:

- A genuinely perceived difference in contract interpretation
  or
- Differences related to the value or timing of payment for goods or services

Summary: Keep talking and trying to settle right up to the door of the courtroom

<u>Working with lawyers</u>

In September 2008, I was privileged to be invited to be a guest speaker by the NSW Law Society in Sydney, in my capacity as executive director of Bilfinger Project Investments in Australia and as a chartered arbitrator. I was probably the only non-lawyer in the room, with an excellent attendance of more than 130 people.

The topic was *'Arbitration from a Commercial Client's Perspective'*, but I took the opportunity to broaden the topic considerably and included quite a bit about what the management of major companies expect from their legal advisors. I prepared the speech very carefully and circulated it to four legal and commercial colleagues in advance for checking, as I wanted to be frank and constructive but not offensive. My colleagues liked the approach, helped me amend it in a few places, and I think spread the word; hence the good attendance.

In summary, my main point in respect to *'working with lawyers'* is that the lawyers should not be left to run the show entirely as they see fit. The client's commercial manager should be working hand-in-glove with the lead lawyer on the case, but amazingly this is not always the situation and client's then wonder later why the case got off the rails and the fees were enormous, often out of proportion to the value of the case.

It seems obvious to me, but the lawyer/commercial manager partnership is the only way to go in a complex commercial dispute, irrespective of whether it will be resolved by arbitration, litigation, adjudication, expert determination, negotiated settlement, mediation, or whatever form of ADR.

The contributions that the lawyer and commercial manager each make are complementary and essential in order to get the optimum result:

Lawyer
- legal and case knowledge
- legal strategy
- proper interpretation of the contract
- separate the emotion from the facts
- objective, cost effective advice

Commercial manager
- status of the issues, claims and disputes
- facts and figures
- corporate objectives
- status of relationships
- implementation of agreed strategy

One point that I did make to my audience of lawyers is that the biggest mistakes they can make are to (a) give *'sitting–on-the-fence'* advice; and (b) string cases out. They will only do it once because they will most probably lose that client altogether when the dust settles and the client realises what has occurred.

Also, it is not uncommon for lawyers who have been involved from the start to give advice that suits their client's commercial objectives (applies to stakeholders and subcontractors) and not a hard-nosed objective interpretation of the contract. This "slanted" advice can prove expensive, both for fees and time wasted. It can actually happen sub-consciously to a degree – again, the human factor.

It is important to remember that big busy corporations like to slot situations into boxes, make provisions in the accounts and get on with life. In most cases they would like the dispute resolved as soon and as inexpensively as possible.

Not always of course, as happened with Seven Network Ltd v News Limited, one of the longest and most expensive cases in Australian history. During the course of the trial the Judge questioned the wisdom of the Claimant continuing to pursue the case and stated that it was *"extraordinarily wasteful"* and *"bordering on the scandalous"* and led him to caution against appealing the decision, which did not deter the Claimant, who appealed and lost, producing a further judgment running to 359 pages. It seems that senior management lost their perspective well and truly.
http://www.australiancompetitionlaw.org/cases/c7.html

My speech "Arbitration from a Commercial Client's Perspective" was published in full by the Chartered Institute of Arbitrators in the UK (CIArb Journal Feb 2009).

A client claimed against a small legal firm for excessive charges over a 5 year period of litigation. Following mediation and the threat of disciplinary proceedings, the legal firm refunded $400,000 fees and suddenly found it was able settle the case and wrap it up within a further 12 weeks, with no further legal fees being charged. The client was an individual, not a corporation, and it was clear the legal firm had been both over-charging and stringing the case out, which was even worse because the client was 92 years old.

Dispute Boards in the context of the ITER Nuclear Fusion Project in France

By Dr Robert Gaitskell QC BSc (Eng.) FIET FIMechE FCIArb
Keating Chambers, London, UK
Barrister, Chartered Engineer, Arbitrator, Mediator, Adjudicator, Expert Determiner

INTRODUCTION

Risk management in the construction industry is the difference between success and failure; between profit and loss; between life and death. The industry itself is inherently risky. I recall some years ago, at the outset of a major project, the project manager called together all the key players and said: *"I know from experience that on a job of this kind it is likely at least one worker will die in an industrial accident. Anyone in this room who won't be able to handle that should leave now."* No one budged, but there were some serious faces in the room after that.

How then do we best manage risk? Careful planning from the outset is crucial. So is taking advantage of techniques that are known to work. One of those techniques is the use of a 'standing dispute board'.

DISPUTE BOARDS

Dispute Boards (DBs) involve a procedure whereby a panel of three engineers/ lawyers (sometimes just one) is appointed often at the outset of the project. Ideally, the DB will visit site three or four times a year and deal with any incipient grievances. This often avoids a complaint crystallising into a dispute. Disputes festering on site are known to sap morale and generate an air of grievance over the whole project. The result is other disputes, strikes, and even accidents.

DB Background

After successful U.S. experience with DBs in the 1960s and '70s, in 1995 the World Bank made the procedure mandatory for all International Bank for Reconstruction and Development (IBRD) financed projects in excess of US$50 million. From 1997 the procedure was adopted by the Asian Development Bank and the European Bank for Reconstruction and Development.

The commonly favoured model for Dispute Boards in the USA was and is the Dispute Review Board (DRB), under which "Recommendations" are issued in respect of the particular dispute being dealt with. This is a relatively consensual approach to dispute resolution. Broadly, if neither party formally expresses dissatisfaction with a recommendation within a stated period of time, the contract provides that the parties are obliged to comply with the Recommendation. If either or both parties do express dissatisfaction within the limited time period, then the dispute may go to arbitration or court litigation. Although the parties may choose voluntarily to comply with a Recommendation while awaiting the decision of the arbitrator or court, there is no compulsion to do so.

FIDIC DB Clauses

FIDIC (the International Federation of Consulting Engineers), with World Bank encouragement, introduced the Dispute Board procedure into its engineering standard forms by way of the 1995 Orange Book form. This was followed by its 1996 introduction into Clause 67 of the Fourth

Edition of the FIDIC Red Book for Building and Engineering Works designed by the Employer. FIDIC adopted the Dispute Adjudication Board model, whereby effect must be given forthwith to a Board decision. If no "notice of dissatisfaction" is issued within 28 days of the Board's decision, it becomes final and binding. If a notice is issued then the matter may proceed to arbitration, although the parties are obliged to comply with the decision in the meantime.

ICC DB Procedure

In late 2004, the International Chamber of Commerce (ICC), Paris, took the process a step forward by launching its Dispute Board Rules, which offered, as part of the menu of procedures available, a hybrid of the two models already referred to. Thus, the ICC scheme offers the conventional DRB and DAB processes, but adds the option of a Combined Dispute Board (CDB), where Recommendations are normally issued, but Decisions may be requested.

Using any of the above procedures the Board is able to fulfil two separate functions:

(a) It can give informal assistance at an early stage with embryonic disagreements, simply by talking through complaints with the parties. The ICC Rules, for example, recognise this aspect of the Board's function in Article 16.

(b) The Board may deal, on a more formal basis, with specific disputes referred to it, giving a determination as required. This is recognised, for example, in Article 17 of the ICC Rules.

It is often the case, obviously subject to the terms of the precise contract appointing the Board, that its formal determinations may be admissible in any subsequent arbitration or court litigation.

Operation of a DB

Two types of Dispute Board need to be distinguished, although they may be used in conjunction with each other. There is the so-called "standing" Dispute Board, where the Board is appointed at the outset of the project and is in place throughout, making periodic visits and dealing with complaints when they first arise, so that, generally speaking, they never develop into disputes. However, on some projects the parties only appoint an "ad hoc" Board when a particular dispute arises. Essentially, this process is akin to simple statutory[1] "adjudication" as widely used in the United Kingdom and various Commonwealth jurisdictions.

Where a standing Dispute Board is used there is an opportunity for the composite Board, consisting of members with both legal and engineering expertise, to walk around the site at regular intervals to see what work has been done. Thus, if subsequently a dispute arises about work which has been covered over, there is a chance the Board will have seen some aspect of that work before it disappeared. In addition to inspecting the site, a typical visit by a Board will involve holding a semi-formal meeting at which all interested parties may air any grievances that they have. The Board, of course, is entirely neutral and independent and will give all concerned a fair opportunity to explain their views.

The precise procedure for any particular Dispute Board will be set out in the contract governing the creation, constitution and activities of the Board in question. It is sometimes the case that the contract will permit separate meetings to be held, so that the Board may meet with one or other party privately in "caucus". It is generally good practice, before this happens, for the matter to be discussed so that both parties know precisely what is contemplated, and agree on the procedure to be followed. If the procedure is not consensual, then there is always the danger that one or other party will feel that things were said at the other party's separate meeting with the Board which ought not to have been said, or which are prejudicial to it and cannot be dealt with since the details are not known.

---

[1] In the UK the initial relevant statute is the 1996 Housing Grants etc. Act. Now see the Local Democracy, Economic Development and Construction Act 2009.

Sometimes the contract will provide that after the site meeting and, ideally, prior to the Board departing, it should produce a short written report for distribution to all concerned. This would record the attendees and details of the meeting, what was seen on the site visit, any grievances raised, and any determinations (whether Recommendations or Decisions) made. Future action required of the parties (e.g. the production of documents for the next meeting), and an explanation of what the Board itself will be doing, if anything, prior to the next meeting, should also be noted in the report. The proposed date for the following visit can also be identified.

Ordinarily, a Standing Board will remain in place until the conclusion of the project, which is often marked by, for example, a Certificate of Practical Completion or some equivalent document.

My experience of standing DBs is that they work: they really do stop all or most complaints crystallising into disputes that need expensive arbitration or litigation. Often the dynamics of why they work can be intriguing. I was once chairing a dispute board in Asia, where we went to site regularly. Well into the contract an urgent email came from both parties summoning the DB to attend site at short notice since the parties were at war. The three members of the DB dropped what we were doing and flew there in great haste. When we got to the site we were met by both parties, all smiling rather sheepishly. They offered us tea and chatted about the weather (hot). I asked about the urgent summons to deal with the critical dispute. They jointly explained that they had reached a deal and did not require our services on this occasion. They wished us safe flights back. Upon enquiry it emerged that some strange human dynamics had been in play. These were men living and working together in fairly inhospitable terrain. A squabble had blown up and in a flash of temper the DB was summoned. Then both sides appreciated that the DB would arrive and start delving into precisely what was happening on site. The parties did not want outsiders like us to pry into what they considered their private affairs. In order to avoid our investigations they promptly settled the dispute. The result was that we were despatched and they were able to continue constructing the project. They don't teach you that at Harvard Business School.

An exciting job that is using a standing DB is the ITER Fusion for Energy project in the south of France. This aims at demonstrating electricity generation from *"fusion"* rather than from the conventional fission process. This high-value experimental project is supported by a wide range of nations. I ought to emphasize that what I say is all in the public domain – on the project's website, or elsewhere - so you will find no commercial secrets in what follows!

NUCLEAR FUSION

Nuclear fusion is quite unlike nuclear fission. The fission process has, of course, far more public recognition, since that technology lies behind the atomic bomb and conventional nuclear power stations. In the fission process the nucleus of an atom splits into smaller parts, usually producing free neutrons and releasing a very large amount of energy. In a conventional nuclear power station a nuclear reaction is deliberately produced. The fuel rods are bombarded with neutrons and the result is that further neutrons are emitted. This sets up a self-sustaining chain reaction that releases energy at a controlled rate in a nuclear reactor (for a power plant), or at a very high uncontrolled rate (in an atomic bomb). The fission process is linked with nuclear waste problems and with well-known examples of escaping radioactivity (e.g. Chernobyl).

The fusion process, by contrast, is significantly different. At the moment we know a limited amount about the process and are on a steep learning curve. Much of what we do know is very encouraging. Stars, including the sun, experience the fusion process at their cores. The ITER project aims to establish, if it can, that the fusion process may be used to generate electricity on a commercial basis. The process that is to be used involves two fuels which are relatively easily obtained. Deuterium may be extracted from seawater, and Lithium is in the earth's crust. Used together in the fusion process they create Tritium on a significant scale. Ultimately, therefore, the supply of Tritium is potentially unlimited. Mass for mass, the Tritium/Deuterium fusion process envisaged for the ITER Project is expected to release about 3 times as much energy as Uranium 235 fission. Of course, this will be millions of times more energy than any chemical reaction such as burning fossil fuels like oil, gas or coal.

The ecological credentials of fusion include the fact that it emits no pollution or greenhouse gases. Its primary by-product is helium, an inert, non-toxic gas. Unlike fission "melt-down" chain reactions, there is no possibility of a fusion *"run-away"* reaction, since any alteration in the conditions of a fusion reaction results in the plasma cooling within seconds so that the reaction ceases. There is a low waste output.

THE ITER PROJECT

ITER originally stood for the *"International Thermonuclear Experimental Reactor"*. However, nowadays it is generally taken to refer to the Latin word for "the way". The overall budget is now expected, if the prototype proves effective, to approach €16 billion or more. The member states for the project are the EU, which contributes 45% of the cost, and six individual nations, each contributing 9%: India, Russia, China, South Korea, the United States and Japan. The project was first seriously mooted in 1985 at the Geneva Superpower Summit in November of that year.

Broadly, the ITER Project involves about 10 years for the construction of all facilities at Cadarache in southern France, followed by 20 years of operation. If this essentially experimental project is successful, then a demonstration fusion power plant, named DEMO, will follow, introducing fusion energy to the commercial market, by converting the heat generated by the fusion process into electricity in fairly conventional ways familiar to those with an understanding of current power plants.

The broad objective of the ITER Fusion Project is to establish that the reactor, using 50 megawatts of input power, is able to produce ten times as much (500 megawatts) of energy output. Provided that can be achieved for a relatively short period (a matter of minutes) than the principle will have been established and the ultimate success of the DEMO power plant is assured. Another of the key objectives of the ITER Project is to verify that Tritium, one of the necessary ingredients for the process, can be *"bred"* in the reactor, so that the supply of that fuel becomes self-supporting. The technological and scientific challenges involved in the ITER Project should not be under-estimated. Pierre-Gilles de Gennes, the French Nobel physics laureate, once said about fusion: *"We say that we will put the sun into a box. The idea is pretty. The problem is, we don't know how to make the box".*[2]

Plasma

To be successful, the reactor must contain high temperature particles, with their enormous kinetic energy, in a sufficiently small volume, and for a sufficiently long time, for fusion to take place, creating the plasma. Ordinarily protons in each nucleus of the isotope fuel will strongly repel each other, since they each have the same positive charge. However, when the nuclei are brought sufficiently close, with sufficient energy, they are able to fuse. In the ITER Tokomak machine the nuclei are brought close together using high temperatures and magnetic fields.

The plasma in the ITER Tokamak is a hot, electrically charged gas. It is created, at extreme temperatures, by electrons separating from nuclei. About 80% of the energy produced in the plasma is carried away from the plasma by the neutrons which, having no electrical charge, are unaffected by the constraining magnetic fields. These neutrons then hit the surrounding walls of the Tokamak, and are absorbed by the blankets on the walls and so transfer their energy to the walls as heat. In the ITER Project this heat is simply dispersed through cooling towers.

However, in the forthcoming DEMO fusion plant prototype the heat generated will be used to produce steam and, through the intermediaries of turbines and alternators, generate electricity.

---

[2] Wikipedia: *"Reactor overview",*

Magnetic Fields

The plasma needs to be heated to 150 million degrees centigrade in the core of the machine. Plasma at that temperature, and with its constitution, cannot be allowed to touch the walls of the reactor, since the plasma would rapidly destroy any constraining vessel and would also cool down, ending the process. Therefore, the plasma is controlled by so-called *"magnetic confinement"*. The plasma is shaped by magnetic fields into a ring, or *"torus"*, and thus it is kept away from the relatively cold vessel walls. These surrounding walls have *"blanket modules"* containing lithium. They are termed *"breeding blankets"* because, as part of the fusion reaction, Tritium can be generated.

The magnetic fields are created using superconducting coils which surround the vessel, while an electrical current is also passed through the plasma. On site at Cadarache the Poloidal Field Coils Winding Facility house has already been completed. It is here that the largest of the magnets will be wound. That particular facility has been designed and constructed by the French consortium Spie Batignolles, Omega Concept and Setec.

The Tokamak Complex

At the heart of the project is the ITER Tokamak machine. This machine draws on the experimental work which broadly stems from a major breakthrough in 1968 when Soviet Union scientists achieved temperature levels and plasma confinement times significantly beyond anything achieved hitherto. The Soviet scientists termed their device, which achieved doughnut-shaped magnetic confinement, a *"tokamak"*. Since then about 200 tokamaks of various kinds, shapes and sizes have been created in research facilities all over the world.

One of the most significant tokamaks is the Joint European Torus (JET) at Culham in England, which has been operational since 1983. JET is a project of EURATOM (the European Atomic Energy Community). The JET tokamak achieved the world's first controlled release of fusion power in 1991[3]. The ITER tokomak will be twice the size of the largest current machine. It will be housed in the Tokomak Complex at Cadarache. That Complex will include the tokomak machine itself, as well as Diagnostic and Tritium Buildings.

Of particular significance in the construction of that Complex will be the Seismic Isolation Pit, a 17m deep hollow, excavated to house the concrete basemat and the Seismic pads that will protect the buildings and equipment from ground motion in the event of a seismic incident.

Construction activity on site is about to peak, with 3,000 workers present. If all goes according to plan, fusion power should be feeding into the world's electricity grid systems by about 2040.

CONCLUSION

The ITER construction contracts may well make good use of the Dispute Board procedure. Certainly, this procedure has the potential for minimising disputes and dealing with crystallised disputes in a cost-effective way. Risk management involving this sophisticated dispute avoidance procedure is likely to pay for itself and bring a range of benefits in levels of satisfaction among the key players. This will contribute to the timely and efficient completion of one of the world's most exciting energy projects, and benefit us all.

---

[3] ITER website: *"Progress in Fusion".*

Biography – Dr Robert Gaitskell QC

Dr. Gaitskell is the Chairman of the Dispute Board for the ITER nuclear fusion project in France, one of Europe's biggest power ventures. He is a Queen's Counsel., and acts regularly as a Dispute Board Member, Arbitrator, Mediator, Adjudicator and Expert Determinator in construction/ engineering disputes worldwide. He is also a Chartered Engineer, a Fellow of the Institution of Engineering and Technology (FIET), a Fellow of the Institution of Mechanical Engineers (FIMechE), and a Fellow of the Chartered Institute of Arbitrators (FCIArb). As an engineer he was involved in the design of power stations and oil rigs. He is a former Vice-President of the IEE/IET (Europe's largest professional engineering body) and Senator of the Engineering Council and a part-time judge. Dr. Gaitskell is the Editor of "Construction Dispute Resolution Handbook", 2nd ed., May 2011. His PhD, from King's College, London, concerned engineering standard form contracts. He is the Chairman of the IET/IMechE Joint Committee on Model Forms, which produces the MF/1-4 Suite of Contracts (used for power plants and other infrastructure projects).

Dr Gaitskell practices in Keating Chambers, London, UK

Understanding and Managing Difficult Client/Contractor Relationships

By David Somerset BSc LLB(Hons) FRICS, FCIArb MEWI
Managing Director Somerset Consult UK

The Stages of a Client/Contractor Relationship on a Construction Project

Construction projects are similar to a marriage, in terms of relationships. A large percentage of construction projects end up with a strained relationship between the parties.

At tender stage, much like a courting period, each party is in a happy state of mind to make concessions to forge a relationship. The project starts and shortly thereafter, so do the niggles. These niggles escalate into complaints which increase exponentially as the construction works advance. The relationship at this point is rocky but still retrievable. On completion of the works the final account and claims arrive. This generates diametrically opposed views of the contractor's entitlement.

The ideal situation (as recommended for any marriage guidance) would be to try and resolve the differences. Sadly, this is not always the way, and emotions and principles blur realism. In this event, the parties turn to the lawyers (and/or claims consultants). After much time, effort and stress, a third party decides on the matter.

Why can Construction Projects not conclude with all Parties being content?

Procuring a construction project is (with few exceptions) not the same as purchasing a product, for example, a car. Construction is by nature, unique. Projects are normally a one-off with issues regarding buildability, time and cost. Add to this consultants who may have not worked together and have different interests. Whilst much can be done in the form of risk assessments and regular reviews to monitor the performance of the project, often human relationships should be considered, in particular that of the client (and rightly so as he is the buyer).

It would be rare for a client who decides to build to start off with a negative state of mind that he will fall out with the contractor and/or consultants. However, once a client has negative niggles these can develop into more extreme emotions. For example, in the case of *Walter Lilly Company v Mackay,* the client Mackay became highly emotional and fell out with the contractor and consultants to his detriment (this being an extreme case).
www.bailii.org/ew/cases/EWHC/TCC/2012/1773.html

Problems will invariably occur on a project for which the parties will seek to blame each other. However, an understanding of the client is paramount. If the client becomes awkward and withholds payment, this invariably has a domino effect. The main contractor is then likely to hold off paying sub-contractors and goodwill and trust become strained and exacerbate the already sensitive situation.

Experience shows that where clients are carefully managed and do not feel they are being taken advantage of then this leads to a successful project. This is easier said than done and each project depends on its own circumstances.

To address the human factor, the Royal Institution for Chartered Surveyors and the Association of Project Managers have jointly commissioned a Stakeholder Guidance note that seeks to provide advice for anyone encountering 'human' as well technical challenges in their working lives. The Guidance note sets out ten key principles, namely:

i. Communicate
ii. Consult, early and often
iii. Remember: they're only human
iv. Plan it
v. Relationships are key
vi. Simple, but not easy
vii. Just part of managing risk
viii. Compromise
ix. Understanding what success is
x. Take responsibility

The Guidance note provides a useful insight into those seeking to improve relationships on a project.

http://www.rics.org/de/knowledge/journals/construction-journal/construction-journal-june-july-2014/

Case Study of a Project with Wealthy Foreign Clients

The material of this case study follows a similar pattern to a number of projects for wealthy foreigners carried out in the London area in the last few years.

The client purchased a property in London and then proceeded to appoint a professional team including an interior designer.

The client required a fit-out of the property to a bespoke luxury apartment.

These types of projects are unique but this one followed a familiar pattern. My experience of the project was as follows:

The client purchased the London property without much consideration and advice from professionals. It required an extensive fit-out and a French interior designer was appointed, together with other consultants.

With an incomplete design, tenders were sought on a two-stage tender procedure and a contractor was appointed. A cost plan was prepared by the quantity surveyors based on similar projects, albeit that at the high end of the market. There are very few comparable projects and the costs all depended on the final selection of finishes.

The contractor, having been appointed, set out a program for the Works on the assumption that the specialist packages would be issued in a timely manner.

The First Issue - This arose in respect to the specialist packages. The interior designer insisted on non-competitive tenders from specialist contractors (most of these being French). The package tenders were vastly in excess of the Cost Plan allowance but moreover, because of the language difficulties, were not particularly easy to reconcile in terms of the Scope of Works/Rates.

The Second Issue - Once the specialist sub-contractors were appointed, they acted as if they were in contract with the interior designer and paid lip service to the main contractor. Changes were being claimed for which the main contractor and the quantity surveyor were unaware of and resulted in an upward movement of the Cost Plan.

The Third Issue – Due to the upward movement of the Cost Plan, the interior designer was invited to attend the meetings to explain the changes. The interior designer played the game well and explained why the change was necessary and the cost was what one can expect if one required a bespoke apartment. The client in most instances agreed with the additional cost, albeit some of the costs were exorbitant. This meant the Quantity Surveyor had minimal control of the costs.

The Fourth Issue - The project fell into delay as the time allowances for the specialist sub-contractors was not sufficient and given the numerous changes. Extensions of time were awarded by the Contract Administrator. However, the client was adamant that the project was to be completed by a certain date and would not accept anything less.

The Fifth Issue – It is a fact that specialist works, including artistic decorations, if rushed will result in the works not being perfect and having numerous defects. The main contractor, endeavouring to complete the Works, pushed and coerced the specialist sub-contractors to complete, which was achieved. However, from a quality perspective, the Works were disappointing and contained many defects.

The Sixth Issue - By the time the Works achieved Practical Completion (albeit there was an extensive defects schedule), the main contractor had submitted a sizeable claim for loss and/or expense. The client, having spent considerable sums on changes, failed to understand the concept of claims. In their mind this was not tangible (as opposed to a change) and they would not entertain any kind of settlement. This was mirrored downstream to the specialist sub-contractors. The result was a stand-off between the client and the main contractor and with the specialist sub-contractors refusing to attend to the defects until there was some recognition (and payment) of their claims.

The Seventh Issue - The main contractor refused to rectify the defects given that the client refused to entertain any claims. To resolve the situation a settlement was done whereupon an amount was deducted from the final account in respect of the defects. The deduction for rectifying defective works was offset by the main contractor against the respective specialists.

The Eighth Issue - Generally works carried out by others can, at a price, be rectified by others. However, in the situation of specialist works, for example specialist artistic works, stone etc., this is much more difficult. The client was then faced with a difficult situation of employing the same specialist sub-contractors (as originally employed by the main contractor) to rectify the defects. In many cases, the client was held to ransom and paid excessive sums to rectify the Works.

The lessons learnt from this case are as follows:

(i) Wealthy clients normally expect to get what they want. In addition they want the best, with construction projects being no different. The Cost Plan needs to reflect this;

(ii) They are normally swayed by the charisma and promises of the interior designers and others who can offer bespoke products;

(iii) When an interior designer is appointed on a luxury property, they will often try and make a name for themselves and seem oblivious to time and cost issues. This needs to be factored into the program and Cost Plans. However, a tighter contract with the interior designer may constrain some of the excesses;

(iv) These types of clients never take kindly to claims and never think they have done anything wrong. However, they are normally content to pay for changes which are tangible. Therefore, include for additional preliminaries in the cost of variations;

(v) Always seek to appoint local specialist sub-contractors (as opposed to foreign specialists) as this avoids cultural and language issues;

(vi) Recognise that timescales for specialist sub-contractors are considerably greater than for normal sub-contractors and that they cannot be rushed, and finally,

Always seek to please the client and do not make them feel threatened, even if they are wrong. They can be very obstructive and have deep pockets to fund any dispute.

Biography - David Somerset

David is a director of Somerset Consult (based in London), a claims, disputes and legal support services consultancy specialising in construction and engineering projects. David is a Chartered Surveyor and also holds a Law Degree.

David specialises in mechanical and electrical works and has produced a number of articles relating to design responsibilities and costing information.

David has been appointed as an Independent Expert on numerous large projects (UK and internationally) ranging from large commercial developments, hospitals to power stations. He is advisor to a number of large organisations in the UK regarding procurement strategy and claims management.

www.somersetconsult.com

Narrative: 'A Typical Negotiation at a Claims Settlement Meeting'

Attendees:
> The Employer (EMP)
> The Contractor (CTR)
> The Independent Negotiator (IND)

IND: *We will now move on to Variation Claim No. 37, which is for $1.35m for 300m² of additional area added to the ground floor. Mr CTR, could you please provide details in support of your claim?*

EMP: *There is no point. We refuse to pay this ridiculous claim. $1.35m is an outrageous amount; we never gave approval for this expenditure in advance as required under the Contract; the work took 6 months longer than it should have and there is a long list of defects; and on top of all that they are also claiming an EOT and daily costs, obviously trying to double up on a lot of the costs. This claim is not debatable and should be withdrawn.*

CTR: *You instructed us to carry out the work. It is a totally valid claim.*

EMP: *We requested a quote for the work, but we never confirmed it in writing and you proceeded anyway. It was at your risk and you can wear it. End of discussion as far as we are concerned.*

IND: *Can we just take this quietly please? It seems that we have **a number of issues here – the validity of the claim; the quantum; the time to complete the work; the defects; and the EOT and daily costs claim.***

I would like to take it one step at a time with these issues and clearly the first thing to establish is whether or not it is a valid claim. Are we in agreement on this?

EMP: *It's a waste of time, but reluctantly yes.*

CTR: *Agreed, but there is also another complication to this claim that we want to include in the discussion. When we finalised the scope of works for this additional work the EMP requested that we leave out the FF&E because they want to manage it themselves under a direct subcontract. That is fine, but at the same time the EMP advised that **they wish to omit the FF&E for all of the West Wing from our Contract and take over our subcontractor on a directly managed basis.***

*Under the terms of the Contract they **cannot do this without our agreement** and if we agree, which we haven't at this stage, **we are entitled to reimbursement for overheads and loss of profit.***

EMP: *Typical! Now you are trying to hold us to ransom at the same time!*

IND: *Mdme and gentlemen. Let us take this quietly please and work our way through it all in a methodical way in accordance with the contractual rights and obligations of each of you.*

Mr CTR, can you please tell us why you think your claim is valid?

CTR: *When we got the request for a quote there wasn't even a schematic design or sketch drawing of what was required, no details whatsoever; no layout or specification, no M&E*

requirements or finishes, nothing, just a general request for another 300m² to be built on the end of the West Wing. We noted all this in our letter of 12 July and said that for these reasons we could not provide a firm quote at that stage, but we would be prepared to undertake the work in accordance with the Schedule of Rates in the Contract and in the event of items not covered in the Schedule we would provide supporting evidence of the costs, plus the overheads and margins as stated in the Particular Conditions of the Contract. We offered to work up the design and specifications with the client. Your letter of 17 July confirmed we should proceed on that basis.

EMP: We said proceed with the design and specifications, but we didn't say proceed with the work. We still wanted to know what the end cost would be and if any complications would arise from the design.

CTR: We completed the design and specifications in consultation with your people and gave it to you in early October. At the Site Meeting on 14 October your representative accepted it all and told us to proceed with the work in accordance with Schedule of Rates and the terms of our letter of 12 July. This is all in the Minutes.

EMP: That person no longer works for us and he had no authority to tell you to proceed on that basis and we also didn't get a copy of the Minutes for a long time after you started. In any event our representative made it a strict condition that you had to complete the work and hand it over to us for fit-out within 120 days, but you took 210 days. We didn't give you written confirmation on our letterhead. Mr IND, the claim is not valid; they did it at their risk and in any case it probably only cost them a fraction of what they have claimed, which is a spit in the ocean in a $260m project. They haven't complied with the Contract processes and we are not paying for it.

CTR: Mr IND, there is more. Firstly the Minutes were emailed to the EMP the day after the meeting, on 15 October. This is a copy of the email. Secondly, on 17 October we wrote letter Ref. 1710 confirming that we were proceeding in accordance with the terms of our letter of 17 July that set out the basis for the costs to be charged. The letter was hand delivered to the EMP together with a Transmittal Note, which was signed by the EMP's receptionist and this is a copy. During the construction the EMP inspected the site on 6 occasions, which are all noted in the site diary. Clearly the EMP accepted the works and the cost basis.

IND: Mdme EMP, from the evidence provided it is my view that this is a valid claim and I recommend that you accept it as such and that we move on to the next issue with this claim. However, before discussing the quantum I would like to understand why the work took 210 days instead of the 120 days that was agreed in the Minutes of the Site Meeting on 14 October, because this may have an impact on the quantum calculations.

CTR: This is simple. Three weeks after we started the whole of the West Wing was put on hold for 90 days because the EMP was considering a much larger addition than the 300m² that we are talking about. This was also recorded in the Minutes of each weekly Site Meeting until the "hold" was lifted. We kept asking what was going on, but weren't involved at all or asked to price anything. Don't forget that the rest of the West Wing is almost completed and this 300m² addition has held us up substantially. That is why we are claiming the EOT and daily costs for the whole 210 days; otherwise you will hit us for Liquidated Damages at the end of the day.

EMP: We emphatically disagree that the rest of the West Wing is nearly finished. The 300m² extension is finally finished but the rest of the works won't reach Practical Completion for another 6 months. Without the additional work you would have been late and up for LD's in any case.

IND: *We need to consider the EOT claim as a separate claim on its own merits, but to do this properly it is necessary that the CTR shows in bar chart form just how you suffered overall delay because of the additional 300m²; how you tried to mitigate any delay, which is a contractual obligation; and whether there was any concurrency with the other two EOT claims that I see you have submitted for other works on the West Wing in the period after the 'hold' was lifted. What is also required is a copy of the Master Program as agreed with the EMP prior to proceeding with the 300m², showing when you expected to reach Practical Completion if the EMP had not undertaken the extra 300m².*

Are we all in agreement to put this EOT claim aside for the moment until the CTR has prepared the necessary information?

EMP: *Yes, but we will not be agreeing to any Daily Costs being applied in any event because they are out of proportion to the value of the extra works.*

CTR: *That is not reasonable. The Contract clearly states that the Daily Costs written into the Particular Conditions will apply to all approved EOTs. They are made up of totally different Administrative Costs and Preliminaries to any that we have included in the cost build-up for the 300m² Variation. We agree to prepare the information for the EOT as a separate claim, but we will not consider reducing the Daily Costs.*

IND: *I would like to move on to the quantum please, that is the direct costs of the Variation. Mr CTR, can you please table your breakdown and substantiation of your claim for $1.35m in accordance with Schedule of Rates and your letter of 14 July. I would like to point out that it would have been helpful if this had been provided in advance as you had agreed, so that the EMP had some time to consider it before today's meeting.*

CTR: *Yes, we have it here. We did not supply it in advance because we only finished it last night. There was an error in the calculations and the amended total is $937,000. Of this, $263,000 is not covered by the Schedule of Rates, but the invoices from the suppliers and subcontractors are all here. And we got three quotes for everything.*

With regard to the defects, the EMP is well aware that they have now all been rectified and signed-off by the TA.

EMP: *We will need to have a close look at all that, but we don't agree you should get the Contract amount for overheads and margin for this extra work. You haven't employed any extra staff to do the work and you are doing very well out of this Contract anyway. Actually, we are very disappointed by your change of attitude to our project. You have become very pedantic about imposing the terms of the Contract. When we started you made a lot of noise about being easy to deal with and having a 'give and take' approach to avoid claims and disputes, but now it seems to be all 'take' and no 'give'. How about reverting to your original idea and showing some good faith!*

CTR: *Your payments are nearly always late; you put parts of the project on hold and procrastinate on decisions; you make changes and don't want to pay for them; in short, you want us to take all the risks and not make a margin on anything. We are a construction company, not your bankers. Our suppliers, subcontractors and employees expect their money to be paid on time and we do this. If we lose money on each job we will go broke and so will some of our subbies and a lot of people will lose their jobs. Where's the good faith!*

At the same time you want our agreement to omit $2.6m of FF&E for the West Wing from our Contract, after we have done all the hard work obtaining the quotes and getting it all organised. This work is due to start 2 weeks from today, on Monday 20th, so we want our Variation claim and the EOT and Costs sorted out this week on a reasonable basis, otherwise no agreement on omitting the FF&E. And we want reimbursement for the overheads and loss of profit on the rates stipulated in the Contract.

IND: *Mdme EMP and Mr CTR, I would like to recommend the following in order to resolve all these issues.*

> *- Time is of the essence because the FF&E is due to start in two weeks.*

> *- If possible, the CTR should prepare the EOT information so that we can meet again to review it by the end of this week. In doing this it is important that you can demonstrate that the days being claimed are non-concurrent and that the days claimed for the actual work could not have been done simultaneously with the other continuing works, as distinct to the days claimed for the 'hold' on the works.*

> *- At the same time, during this week it would be good if the EMP could review the revised quantum for the Variation claim.*

> *- In regard to the overheads and margin for the Variation claim, these items were included in the Contract by agreement for just this sort of situation so I think it is reasonable that they be allowed by the EMP and that you should comply with the terms of Contract. The CTR may not have employed extra staff for this additional work, but the existing staff still had to do the work.*

> *- In regard to the application of the Daily Costs to any EOT that you might agree it is my view that the CTR has an obligation to show that you have encountered extra costs or suffered loss due to the time taken for this extra work. I say this because the Contract is somewhat ambiguous in the terms relating to the application of Daily Costs to days awarded for extension of time. It is not clear that this situation in respect of Variations was the intention of the parties or in contemplation when you signed the Contract.*

    On this basis, I would like to resume this meeting next Friday at 8.30am. Do you agree with this?

CTR: *Yes, we will be ready by then.*

EMP: *Yes, we can do that but I can't see how we can resolve everything. We are too far apart.*

IND: *I have observed that generally the relationship between you both has been very good and cooperative and in the right spirit to deliver a first class project. The two issues that you are having difficulty with are the omitting of the FF&E and the application of the EOT daily costs. I think it is very much in the interest of both parties to reach an amicable commercial agreement, maybe with some compromise from each of you.*

    Remember that there is still 18 months to run on this project and to date you have not had a single formal dispute. And I would also like to point out that if you cannot reach agreement and end up in arbitration, the resolution will be delayed for a considerable time, probably 12 to 18 months; the EMP will not be able to take over the FF&E works; the costs of the arbitration will be out of proportion to the real amount in dispute as of today and the time involved in running with the arbitration will be very considerable.

    In summary this would put considerable strain on your otherwise excellent relationship and I really do not think this is a good alternative to reaching an amicable settlement at the end of this week.

EMP: *We couldn't agree more and we will come to the meeting on Friday keeping that in mind.*

CTR: *Thank you and we will do the same.*

**Remember that whenever there is a problem
with a project it can invariably be traced back to
a breakdown in communication somewhere.**

Techniques for Negotiating Settlements

Negotiating settlements is an area in which I have specialised for many years as an independent negotiator and for which I have received appointments from government authorities and corporate entities.

My philosophy and firm policy has always been to use all possible avenues to achieve fair and reasonable settlement of claims and disputes through negotiation, rather than through the courts, arbitration, adjudication and expert determination. My approach is different to mediation and conciliation in that it is much more proactive. It has proven to be very successful.

As an independent settlements negotiator I have come across many situations where clients and contractors are at loggerheads and communications between them are such that the only way forward appears to be through formal dispute proceedings.

I put together the narrative in Chapter 25, based on a typical settlement negotiation, to show how a calm analytical approach with a bigger picture perspective can resolve differences and arguments over claims.

When serious differences arise between the parties over claims or other contractual matters, it is best to never call them disputes unless they actually end up in formal dispute proceedings, because the word 'dispute' has a negative connotation that sets the wrong scene for a negotiation.

To me they are just issues and there is nearly always a way to resolve them through negotiation. An interesting philosophy to adopt is to say to yourself *'this issue will be resolved by 5 years from now one way or another, so let's find a way for the parties to resolve it now'* and then work patiently with them to find that way.

This sort of negotiation is more than a traditional mediation in that the negotiation process is very proactively led by the independent negotiator, but first you have to win their confidence that you are experienced in the subject under debate and that you will be objective, completely impartial and fair and reasonable in the advice you put forward.

Even when the parties have reached an apparent stalemate, ceased communicating and have resorted to firing bullets at one another through their lawyers it is not too late to negotiate, although it may be difficult to get them in the same room to start talking.

A typical example of this sort of situation is described at the end of this chapter in *'Paddy's Market, Haymarket, Sydney, – a classic failure to communicate'.*

As another example, with one project I acted as the independent negotiator and chaired settlement meetings on more than 100 disputed construction and EOT claims, many of which were extremely complex, but we agreed settlement on 90% of them. The negotiations took more than one year and some of the claims took several months. The parties, who were from three different countries, were keen to avoid long and costly international arbitration so there was a willingness to compromise, which is an extremely important factor for success. The process used was far more proactive than mediation. I was requested by the Employer, the Contractor and the Project Manager to use my arbitration experience to analyse each claim and advise my view of the likely outcome if the claim ended up in arbitration. The Contract documents were complex and the terms difficult to understand, seeming ambiguous and contradictory in places until you flow-charted the rights and obligations taking into account Precedence of Documents.

I discovered at the outset that the parties had widely different views on the interpretation of the heavily amended FIDIC Contract, so after realising this I put on my arbitrator's hat and wrote an Interpretation and Application of the Contract, including sufficient reference on the rights and obligations of the parties to cover the first batch of claims that were under debate.

So armed with this, we then had further meetings at which the parties presented their cases in detail and I gave my view on what I considered to be the correct interpretation of the Contract, i.e. the likely result if it went to arbitration. With each one I explained my reasons in detail, going through the contractual obligations step by step. With quite a number of the disputes, after I gave my view the parties then took some time to consider the matter further or talk to their lawyers and with most of the claims one party or the other came back with a reasonable settlement offer. Where this didn't happen the first time around we tried again and if still not successful we then parked the claim for a few months and almost every time we did this we reached agreement in the third discussion.

During the overall course of the negotiations, I wrote the following Expert Opinions or indications of likely arbitration findings and issued them to the parties to help them reach settlements:

- *An Opinion on the Interpretation and Application of the Contract Agreement and on the Rights and Obligations of the Parties.*
- *On the Meaning and Application of the Terms of Contract relating to Re-Design by the Contractor.*
- *On the Employer's Entitlement to Reduce the Scope of Work of the Contractor and directly employ and manage subcontractors simultaneously with the Contractor's Works and the cost implications thereof (covering Contract Works, Nominated Subcontractors and Provisional Sums).*
- *On the Contractor's Entitlement to Loss of Profit and Overheads on Omitted Works.*
- *On the Employer's Entitlement to Deduct Counter Claims from the Contractor's Account under the terms of the Contract.*
- *On the Meaning and Application of Amended Terms of Contract relating to Claims for Extensions of Time and Applicable Costs and the respective Contractual Processes.*

I have listed the above examples to demonstrate the importance of really understanding your Contract. Put the time in to do this and get legal advice in doing so; it will save you and your company a great deal of time and cost in managing your claims and disputes, let alone a lot of frustration and sleepless nights.

Paddy's Market, Haymarket, Sydney – a classic failure to communicate

The markets have been operating for 150 years and accommodate more than 800 stalls. The markets are managed by a government authority that works in conjunction with the Stallholder's Association. In 1987 a property developer obtained the re-development rights and a long-term lease to the site from the government, with a view to putting a 35 level multi-storey building on top of re-configured markets and a podium of conventional retail and cinemas.

The new architectural plans were submitted for Planning Approval and put on public display, but up to this time the developers and their design team had not met and consulted with the Stallholder's Association at all. The Stallholders were incensed because the plans took no account of the original stall and product locations, the people and goods flow or the loading docks. Of particular concern were the stall locations and sizes, because these related to their leasehold goodwill value. Typically, the values of the stalls ranged from $100,000 to $250,000 at that time and were real assets.

The developers had also agreed with the government to temporarily relocate the Markets for 3 years to some disused railway sheds 2 kilometres away, again without any consultation with the Stallholders.

The Stallholder's Association responded with Court injunctions to prevent the Planning Approval, the temporary move and the development as a whole. The injunctions resulted in a stalemate for 18 months, at which time I was asked by the developers to act as mediator. The stallholders were suspicious of my role, but agreed to a meeting of all parties, with two representatives each. At the meeting I quickly confirmed that there still had not been any contact between the developers and the Stallholders, except through their lawyers. The first meeting was fiery and the Stallholders walked out after 10 minutes. The second meeting one week later was similar, but I was able to exchange personal phone numbers with the Stallholder's President. We then met informally over some lunch, following which I had some useful meetings with the Stallholder's Committee at which they explained their concerns. From this I was able to convince the developers that their plans were completely impractical for a number of reasons. They re-briefed their architects and design team to start again, this time working in close consultation with the Stallholders. After 4 months everyone agreed on the redesign and the logistics for the temporary relocation. I attended most of the initial re-design meetings to make sure that everyone was communicating and staying on track.

The Stallholders cancelled their legal proceedings and Planning Approval was granted. At this stage the developers sold out to another property company. The lengthy delay had burdened them with too much holding cost. The new owners simplified the podium and raised the multi-storey by several levels and eventually completed a successful development.

The risk management lesson here is very obvious - a little communication goes a long way. It is the easiest form of risk management, but breakdowns in communication probably cause more problems than anything else.

Happy ending – I was guest of honour at the Stallholder's next Christmas dinner, with around 2,000 guests at the party.

The Case for Independent Audits of Major D & C Projects

Independent project audits are a very cost effective and prudent form of risk management:

- They are broader based than internal audits or Dispute Review Boards (DRB)
- They provide early warning alerts for potential issues
- They can cover all claims and disputes (DRB issues) as well

The audit team should work closely with site management with the prime objective being to prevent projects running into trouble.

The real value of independent audits comes from starting them early in the project life and conducting them at least every 4 months, reviewing all aspects of the contract, with recommendations made for corrective actions to mitigate if problems are found.

The scope should be agreed with the client, including all basic areas which might put the project at risk:

- Design development and cost planning
- Progress v program; expediting measures
- Drawdowns v budget & program
- Cash flow management and financial reporting
- Costs-to-complete
- Project reporting
- Site resources capacity and capability, including key people suitability, staffing levels, consultants, plant and equipment
- People management, team spirit and employee satisfaction
- Subcontract status and management, including their payments
- Compliance with contractual obligations
- Specification compliance
- Planning, Building & Authority Approvals
- Issues at large, claims and disputes
- Communications and relationship management
- Meetings and documentation discipline
- Environmental requirements
- Health & Safety procedures & standards
- Quality Assurance
- Corporate Governance
- Completion and commissioning plans
- Staff compliance with the "First to know" rule for the project director

The team should start with design development and cost planning as this combined process is the most critical phase of a D&C project; when you make or break a D&C project. These two processes must be run in parallel. It is pointless having the design consultants develop the design unless there is constant cost checking, with comparison to the budget or bid price. This is when independent peer reviews are most valuable. They have proven to be very effective and valuable in the design process.

After a successful design development and cost plan phase it should then be a matter of efficient head contract and subcontract management and tight program control, subject to the usual types of variations and the weather. But this is oversimplifying it, especially with PPP contracts where project managers commonly don't understand the obligations of the different parties and the implications and liabilities arising from the contract and therefore they often don't realise they are getting into trouble.

All of this is based on two major assumptions of course:

- That the estimators got it right in the first place and the directors have not chopped too much out to win the Bid
- That the Bid passed all the risk management checkpoints and red reviews and was thoroughly checked for potential risks

Major construction companies generally say they have these processes in place with their internal audit team and therefore don't need external audits, but they still have projects that get into trouble.

However internal audits tend to:

- Not look at the bigger picture
- Check historical figures
- Not critically examine forward programs, resources and costs-to-complete
- Have loyalty or conflict of interest issues
- Not be completely independent and objective

It is not always easy to convince construction managers that they benefit either way from external audits. The audits should be seen as "safety first" low cost risk management. If explained properly to project directors they should be welcomed, because it becomes a 'win-win' situation for them.

- The upside is confirmation that everything is healthy and on track
- Alternatively, if the external audit team unearths some problems and they are corrected or mitigated before they get out of hand then the project director still gets the credit
- If an innovative solution suggested by the audit team saves time and cost, the project team still gets the credit
- The fees are highly cost effective in proportion to project value

Pride and egos can be major barriers to having independent audits accepted by senior on-site managers, but 'it's too late to try and shut the gate after the horse has bolted'.

> **The question is how to convince several very head-strong, stubborn project managers that they should be identifying, capturing, tracking and mitigating risk.**

Independent audits can be undertaken by:
- The client to overview the entire project
- The head contractor
- A major subcontractor
- A principal consultant
- Any combination of the above

The independent audit team must have extensive experience in

- A wide range of major projects
- Design development/cost planning
- International forms of contract
- Contract management & cost control
- Performance programming & expediting
- Operations & asset management
- ADR and QS processes

So what point of difference do independent audits really offer in respect of risk management?

- Team members have the experience to *"smell"* issues in the making and provide early warning
- They will make their own assessment – irrespective of reports and programs from the project team
- The approach is hard-nosed and objective on current status combined with strategic look-ahead

---

Starting early is the key to success and the cost is really minimal

---

The Value of Independent Oversight

By John Messenger
Director, Driver Trett Group

The need for independent review

If construction, and in particular infrastructure, now involves much greater levels of 'partnership' between client and contractor/service provider, then relationship management is going to have to be the central pillar around which the partnership is developed and maintained.

Relationship management at this level is still a developing skill set beset by issues most of which represent limitations of the mind/human dynamics rather than insurmountable problems. At the root of most of these issues is the process of competitive bidding which, although important for governance and the basis for providing good value for money, largely prevents the basis for developing the underpinnings of partnership and relationship management before the commercial and contractual basis is locked in. Faced with the need for a competitive process most clients and bidders focus on the bid process and leave the issues of relationship management to be dealt with afterwards. Even among the more experienced clients and private sector companies few have developed systems which cater for the kind of long term relationships that infrastructure provision creates.

Partnership does not mean ignoring the fundamental conditions of the contract and the contractual relationship or a blurring of the responsibilities. Clients must always be responsible for the implications of changing their requirements and contractors must always be responsible for the mistakes they make in estimating resources and costs and for any failings in delivery. Each party has to meet their obligations and take responsibility for the risks which are theirs to take under the contract.

A focus on partnership does however mean joint responsibility for the management and hence the success or failure of the enterprise. Relationship management is then the process by which the partnership is maintained, especially in times of difficulty. Independent review is the means by which an impartial view is taken of the various stages/elements of the project and which informs both sides of the partnership of issues which need to be addressed to keep the project on course.

Claims and disputes are predominantly borne out of poorly defined requirements, uncontrolled change processes and poor project administration. How much better therefore to sort out the details of the partnership and the means for maintaining it before the contract locks in conditions which hinder or prevents it.

Most infrastructure contract agreements incorporate some form of independent audit and dispute resolution provisions to assist in the administration of the contract. These services can be provided by a number of bodies set up (at various times) for a specific purpose or stage (e.g. Dispute Resolution Boards) or are sometimes combined into an 'independent engineer' appointment. Whilst these arrangements address the requirement to administer particular contractual obligations and ensure that the contract can be implemented as written they have the following inherent failings:

- The independent element does not provide for establishing and fostering of partnership relations; rather it looks to obviate the need for the parties to collaborate and is focussed on a legalistic approach.

- The presence of an officially appointed independent body encourages an abdication of responsibility by partner representatives who become reactive instead of proactive and the gap between the partnering organisations widens instead of closing.
- None of the provisions cover the conceptual, development and procurement negotiation stages.
- In practice the independent party's service package is also likely to have been tendered and hence the independent party has their own interests and contract terms in mind, which will rarely be aligned with the immediate needs and interests of the partner organisations.

The importance of independence in reviews is to ensure impartiality which can be accepted by both sides of the partnership but, even more importantly, independence provides the 'second pair of eyes' which see things that have been missed and also a defence against the build-up of politically motivated agendas and positions. It enables everyone to maintain balance and a sense of perspective and it avoids unjustified views from prevailing. In all cases however an independent review/audit should be in support of the partner relationship and not a replacement for it.

The remainder of this section is written around partnership arrangements for large scale infrastructure projects; a lot of the material might however be equally applicable to smaller projects in which clients and contractors share the risk in the development of the design and construction works.

<u>Implications of the competitive process</u>

If we are to avoid the problems of 'back-fixing' partnership and relationship management measures we need a way of ensuring more active engagement at an early stage and we need a means of carrying it forwards.

A means of examining the joint benefits from collaboration on the fundamental aspects of the business might then be possible including:

- Cost reduction
- Profit sharing
- Risk allocation and mitigation

A clear understanding of these issues and a joint approach to them would then form the foundation of the relationship rather than the divide created by the contract.

Earlier attention to these key issues in the development of partnership arrangements is undoubtedly desirable but will require a significant shift in attitudes towards the bidding process before it can be provided for effectively. In essence we need to close the gap between client and contractor that inevitably exists at the outset and might be summarised as:

Clients:

- must have competition which complies with applicable legislation and must be able to show probity and adherence to 'rule and regulations'
- want to offload risk in order to create reliable forward cost budget
- must show that they have obtained best value for money
- want to ensure that they obtain a solution/service provision that they are comfortable with and which will operate at a satisfactory level and be reliable

Clients, who are frequently beset by procurement rules which effectively demand a hands-off approach in order to avoid allegations of impropriety, currently tend to regard the tender process as a hazard to be dealt with by avoiding contact with Bidders altogether. This leads to client defined procurement processes which rely on the bid documentation, limited interaction beyond written exchanges and a focus on obtaining strictly 'like for like' bids which allow easy assessment and comparison (often whilst emphasising an interest in 'innovative bids').

It is therefore comfortable for clients to believe that they can demand anything that they wish in a project brief, specification or contract and bidders will be bound to comply and bid on those terms. A more realistic matching of project requirements to the ways in which industry is structured and in which bidders and funders perceive the risks would increase the levels of competition and the chance of successfully finding an ideal partner.

Bidders:

- must be able to see that the bidding process will be fair and that they will have an equal chance of success as other bidders
- must be able to assess the business case and assess the return on investment and the business risks

Bidders know the cost of bidding major projects and look for indications that the opportunity will fit within their chosen scope of activities and that the client will be reasonable to deal with. The idea that bidders flock to compete for any opportunity that is presented to them is no longer sensible and the dangers of dealing with those that do not consider these matters must be obvious. Faced with a lack of information, or a client who will not communicate usefully, leads bidders into a strategic approach which limits the cost of initial bid preparation in a gamble to achieve *'preferred bidder'* status.

The traditional client approach of remaining strictly detached from the bidders during the bid period simply does not provide a basis for developing the partnership. Lobbing a tender enquiry out to open tender and restricting the timescales for bidding are profoundly counter-productive. Bidders need time to assemble their teams and to address what are often complex requirements. A careless attitude towards the market place and lack of time to bid is always indicative of a badly managed process and engenders fears that the procurement process has been rigged to favour particular bidders; such things will deter many potential competitors from offering bids.

The traditional contractor approach of keeping bid costs down and putting in the absolute minimum effort necessary until they have an indication that their bid is being considered simply does not work in a situation in which a partnership relationship has to be developed.

Partnership and competitive tendering may therefore appear to be fundamentally incompatible; however joint interest represents a key to the problem. Both sides have an interest in delivering a successful project and the difference between a deliverable project and non-starter lies in the development of an optimal solution and control of costs (unnecessary work-scope, unwarranted levels of specification, risks and uncertainties add cost, joint solutions remove it).

Bringing the parties together within a competitively tendered situation during the pre-contract stages is difficult, however there are procurement methods which address these issues (two stage tendering, the inclusion of 'preferred bidder' stages, etc.). More enlightened approaches are possible and processes which provide for early dialogue/involvement with potential bidders develop from time to time in various countries. These methods may not yet be accepted in many places, however the ideas and approaches may be incorporated in ways which encourage the development of partnership conditions but which maintain the core principles of competitively procured services.

The need to develop a project prospectus and to actively market projects is understood by some but does not seem to be accepted by many clients. Marketing projects is highly beneficial as it provides information which allows the project to be tailored to suit the limitations of the market place and it maximises the competition by encouraging potential bidders to come forward and joint venture teams to assemble.

Introducing a marketing stage in the project development cycle may seem to many as the addition of a delay in the project timescale. If the marketing work is undertaken whilst the feasibility studies and other project documentation are being developed however, the loss of time may be quite minimal.

Systems which permit an engagement with the market place prior to locking down the project details and offering the project for competitive bid are not new and hence a carefully planned and structured marketing stage can provide at least part of the solution to engaging with potential bidders whilst maintaining the requirement for a tender competition.

The development of partnership arrangements for infrastructure projects

Any discussions during the marketing or bidding stage should be as wide as possible. No opportunity should be lost for discussion which allows the two sides to become acquainted with each other and for an examination of the problems that they perceive to exist in the project. Any time spent at this stage can only serve to make later stages easier and to increase the chances of success.

For the early development of potential partnership arrangements the following issues should be addressed:

- An understanding of the basis for joint interest in the project and of what each side wants to get out of the arrangement and how those 'wants' are to be accommodated
- Any 'due diligence' of each other's organisations required to establish that the businesses are sound and that the partnership opportunity is real and will be pursued by each side with full commitment.
- A joint understanding of the key objectives of the project and the criteria by which success will be measured
- A joint discussion of the potential solutions
- A solid understanding of the base business case for the opportunity and of the risks involved in the project and how they will be shared
- A joint discussion of the ways in which competitive process will be administered and assessed
- An understanding of the project documentation including the specification and the contract and the implications of key provisions on risk and price

Review requirements for particular project stages

Independent review/oversight is then the means by which an impartial overview is taken of the various stages/elements of the project and which supports the maintenance of the overall enterprise and partnership. Higher level project governance bodies are frequently put in place by both client and contractor organisations to make key decisions (typically 'steering committees', 'project boards', etc.). These bodies rarely have the ability to properly overview the project with independent 'eyes' and to manage it proactively. Providing a means of undertaking the reviews independently ensures that the potential for hidden agendas is removed and that a wider view and perspective is possible than that which might be produced by personnel who are directly engaged in the project and whose jobs might closely be involved in the outcomes.

Partnership arrangements and the associated relationship management processes clearly develop in line with the stages in the overall life cycle of the project and the focus at each stage can vary widely. The requirements for review and audit therefore need to be tailored to the specific requirements of the various life cycle stages of a project and of the particular flavour of procurement strategy that has been adopted.

Prior to the closure of the contract independent reviews should be undertaken by each side separately.

Bidders are accustomed to providing an independent review of their bid documents prior to submission (typically known as 'red team' reviews), however the effectiveness of bidders review arrangements varies widely. Common problems include:

- Leaving the review until it is too late to rectify any problems
- Inadequate focus on the fundamental business issues

Client organisations rarely undertake any independent review of the early project development stages, perhaps in the belief that their consultants bring that element of independent scrutiny to the work. Regrettably consultants rarely advise clients independently and treat client requirements and instructions as given. Any party which is closely associated with the work is also unable to stand above the whole project and provide the review that is needed to catch problems effectively.

Joint client/contractor independent reviews should be introduced as early as possible in order to encourage the joint understanding of the project and to aid integration of the two sides. Longer term relationships, relationship management processes and the underlying independent review requirements are developing skills and are likely to vary from project to project. An outline of the independent reviews that might be built into any project is shown in the table below.

Review Requirements for Particular Project Stages

Stage	Party Involved	Focus of the Review
Scheme development		*The key focus should be on ensuring that the scope and specification of the scheme/project have been comprehensively established and that it is practical, feasible and viable as a business opportunity. Extraneous requirements, specific solutions and hidden agendas should have been carefully excluded.*
Inception, & project brief	Client and Transaction Advisory Project Management Team	Requirement The review should ensure that the inception and project brief documents represent a fundamental statement of the purpose and objectives of the scheme/project together with the required performance requirements. Key criteria for success should also be identified such that it is clearly evident when the purpose, objective and specified performance standard have been met. The review should ensure that the client's organisation is properly set up and capable of undertaking the development work that the technical work can be undertaken competently. Output/Deliverable The review should confirm that a satisfactory and politically unencumbered project brief has been compiled which states the project objectives and scope requirement without embellishment or pre-conceived ideas as to the solution

Scheme development, feasibility study and prospectus production	Client and Transaction Advisory Project Management Team	**Requirement** The review should ensure that the development process has produced a realistic examination of potential solutions and illustrative scheme layouts which establish that the brief is practical. The output documents should be sufficient for the purposes of project planning, initial approvals, cost estimates and the baseline financial model. The review must ensure that realistic cost, utilisation and revenue forecast modelling has been compiled which establish that the project is financially viable. Leaving any part of this project definition task to potential bidders is likely to prove counter-productive as potential bidders may be deterred by the lack of clear information. **Output/Deliverable** The review should confirm that the requirements of the project brief have been developed into a clear performance specification which leaves the form and operational details to bidders to propose but which makes clear the outputs that are required to meet the client's objectives
Procurement Strategy and Marketing		**The key focus is on ensuring that the project is marketed to potential bidders and that the process of consultation with potential bidders has been comprehensive and that the various issues identified have been incorporated into the project documentation.**
Procurement strategy and process	Client and Transaction Advisory Project Management Team	**Requirement** The review should ensure that a procurement strategy and process has been developed which provides for an engagement with appropriate sections of the market place and which can present a business opportunity that can be picked up by potential bidders that are capable of providing (or developing) competent solutions. The strategy and process should provide for competent assessment and complete probity.
Discussions with potential partner organisations and tender pre-qualification	Client & Concessionaire pre-Relationship Management Team	**Objective** The review should ensure that both client and bidders are provided with an opportunity to comprehensively examine, discuss and comment on the project and the procurement process. **Requirement** Discussions should include a wide examination of the key criteria for success and detailed scope of work. In particular the risks involved in all stages of the project should be examined and agreement arrived at as to how the risk allocation

		might be arranged to maximise the effective joint management of those risks and minimise costs. Bidders should be given an opportunity to examine the possibility of introducing bespoke solutions which innovatively add value to the project. Relationship management should be a specific area of discussion which should lay the groundwork for developing the management systems and procedures which will be carried into the implementation stages.
Confirmation of bidding	Bidders Team	The key bid/no-bid decision will be made at this time and confirmed on issue of the tender documentation. The review should ensure that the bid team have adequately confirmed the following: • The client is serious and that the project will go ahead • The tender process is reliable and fair • The tender period is adequate • The business case has been checked and is viable • A full bidders team has been assembled and secured for the project which is capable of undertaking the full scope of work • Funders are in place • The nature of any qualifications that will need to be attached to the bid
Bidding		*The key focus should be on providing a basis for economic competition which allows for the identification and further development of the most cost effective solution.*
Bid preparation	Bidding Team	Objective Independent bid review is vital to ensure that the bid is comprehensive and that risks and pricing take everything into account.
		Requirement Independent review undertaken throughout the tender period and covering all aspects including: • Contract • Commercial • Technical • Team competence and capacity • Funding • Implementation planning • Programme
Preferred Bidder	Both sides	Particular independent reviews will be needed depending on the details of the procurement strategy and the work to be undertaken during the

		preferred bidder stage. Where the stage includes design development key review requirements will be to confirm that the Project Brief and criteria for success have been met. The preferred bidder stages represent the ideal point at which relationship management processes and combined reviews should be commenced.
Negotiation	Client & Concessionaire pre-Relationship Management Team	Should be seen and arranged as a further extension of the pre-bid discussions
Implementation		***The key focus is on ensuring that the design and construction meet the project brief whilst ensuring that construction risks do not add cost.***
Design and construction	Combined Team	Independent review at regular intervals to ensure the following: Organisation and resources, personnel and systems in place and operational Relationship management processes commenced and delivering combined management of the project Performance monitoring of all aspects of the project
Operations and maintenance		***The key focus moves to service provision and to ensuring that performance targets are met at all times and improved wherever possible through efficient practice.*** ***Relationship management moves to regular review of performance and on ensuring that the project is able to respond flexibly to problems and to changed requirements.***
	Combined Team	Regular independent reviews required to examine the functionality of all aspects of the project including: • Organisation • Personnel • Systems • Monitoring and audit processes and findings • Relationship management processes • 'Fitness for purpose'

There is no substitute for hard experience when it comes to identifying operational inefficiencies and potential project risks

Practical Human Resources Considerations

Personnel Recruitment & Positioning – a different perspective

If you accept my contention that the human aspects of project management are equally or more important than technical skills, then it follows that personal or soft skills should carry significant weight when recruiting personnel, whether it be for long-term employment or short term for a specific project.

I developed the following interview checklist and used it for many years. You will note that it is heavily weighted towards character, personality and personal skills rather than technical skills. By the time an applicant reaches the short list interviews for a job, it is more than likely that their technical skills have been properly checked out and are acceptable, but even if they check out really well it does not necessarily mean this person will be a good team player, be a pleasure to work with and fit into the organisation well.

This check-list should not be tabled during the interview, because that would be too much 'in your face', but make notes on it immediately afterwards as appropriate.

Of course, no one is perfect and allowances nearly always need to be made in respect of some of the personal traits that all of us have.

	Interview Checklist "Fit the Team" Criteria	Comments
1	Experience- specific construction/engineering/PPP	
2	Experience - broad enough & suitable to our company	
3	Experience - specialised enough for the position	
4	Experience – hands-on or academic	
5	Presence generally	
6	Presence at high level	
7	Uncomplicated personality	
8	Eye contact	
9	Open and forthcoming	
10	Listen – and hears – attentive	
11	Talks too much	
12	Talks over the top	
13	Exaggerates	
14	Understates	
15	Alert/sharp witted/street smart	
16	Dress and shoes - neat or sloppy	
17	Knowledge of our company	
18	Energetic/workaholic or 9.00 to 5.00 type	
19	Is this person only looking for a fill-in position	
20	Recreational pursuits	
21	Why moving now/why previous moves	
22	References (for what they are worth)	

23	Work culture expectations	
24	Salary/package expectations	
25	Other interviews recently	
26	Nervousness/adrenalin running (not necessarily a negative)	
27	Overall perception	
28	Would I like to work with this person	
29	Will he/she really fit in and add value to our team	

> **Interviewer** – remember that no one is perfect!
>
> **Interviewee** – *'You never get a second chance to make a good first impression!'*
> **(Will Rogers)**

Egos and Arrogance v. a Team Leader

It is not uncommon to find arrogant managers who fuel their own egos by putting down their underlings. This can be very disturbing and stressful and leave you wondering about your own capabilities, so it is important to not be deterred if you think you are right and have not performed badly. Be patient and sit it out, perhaps talk about it with your peers or human resources manager, as your day will come if you stay focussed on doing your job properly – and so will theirs! Their behaviour is often a cover-up for their inadequacies as managers.

Amazingly, it is also not uncommon that some of these arrogant types also treat personnel from joint venture partners and even clients with rudeness, superiority and disdain, but generally they don't get away with it for long. A few large corporations over the years have fostered this type of behaviour as a company culture, but they are not doing themselves any favours in respect of developing business relationships. It should not be tolerated.

A complete opposite to the above types of managers is the confident and unassuming manager who appoints the best possible people to his team on the basis that their high performance will make their life and workload easier and help them get optimum results, thereby also making them look better in the eyes of those above. There is always the risk in doing this that someone you appoint will outshine you and end up taking your job, but it is a small risk and still worth doing for the sake of the company. Everyone reaches their level of incompetence sooner or later, but it is hard to recognise it in yourself and probably even harder to accept, but if it is your turn then that's life!

> After 4 months of negotiations, the terms of sale of three Australian hotels to a Japanese investor were finalised. Three Japanese executives arrived in Sydney on an overnight flight to formally sign the Sales Contract at a scheduled 9.00am meeting. After polite greetings and introductions the Contract documents were tabled for signature, with the principal Australian signatory being the MD of the hotels division, owned by a larger conglomerate. At this moment the MD's mobile phone rang and he took the call (it should have been switched off). He stood up and walked over to the window overlooking the harbour and talked and talked and talked. Three times his colleagues tried to interrupt him, but he brushed them off. Finally, after 15 minutes he returned to the Board table and just said "let's get on with it, I have a busy day". The Japanese gentlemen, who were clearly annoyed, had a quick discussion, said they wished to defer the signing of the Contract and departed. They sent a polite note later that day withdrawing from the sale.

The MD's behaviour would have been extraordinarily rude and disrespectful to any nationality, but this MD had actually lived in Japan in a senior executive position for a number of years. He lost his job soon thereafter

The Human Fallout from a Failed Project

When projects turn sour the impact can be quite devastating to a wide range of stakeholders and individuals. On the client side the people that conceived and ran the project will likely pay the price, maybe with serious consequences to their careers, unless it is the boss of a private company that made all the wrong decisions, in which case it is his personal pocket that is hurt.

However, that does not prevent contractors, subcontractors, suppliers and individuals further down the chain from suffering the financial consequences. The most evident damage is mostly seen when a head-contractor is terminated for poor performance, has major losses, or even goes to the wall on a series of bad projects, which is not uncommon with small/medium size contractors.

In this situation the people that get hurt most will be the professional consultants, subcontractors and suppliers. Lenders, investors, large construction companies and government authorities take no mercy on the smaller players when these big guys get into trouble, with the result that some of these smaller players may go broke. These larger entities try and protect themselves with specific contractual Agreements tailored for such eventualities, such as Non-Recourse Agreements and Indemnities, but they also commonly write off large sums related to failed projects.

When the smaller businesses suffer losses or go bust as a result of their involvement in a major project that has failed this often results in job losses for many genuine, hard-working people who are far removed from the corporate decision-makers who really caused the problem. These business and job losses can in turn result in people losing their homes and other personal assets and being declared bankrupt.

It is also a well-known fact that unscrupulous property developers and construction head contractors all around the world enter into multiple subcontracts with professional consultants, subcontract specialist trades and suppliers with the specific intent of finding reasons to never pay the last 10% of the subcontract values. Small under-capitalised businesses operating on fine margins cannot survive this for very long, but the unscrupulous bad guys know that there are invariably new subcontractors willing to work for them and take the risk. It is a tough industry in this regard.

Fortunately, this unsavoury practice has drawn the attention of legislators in an increasing number of countries, such as in Australia where the various States have in recent years introduced *'Security of Payments'* legislation which is quite effective in protecting subcontractors from unscrupulous employers.

Decision Making for Survival and the Inherent Risks

It is entirely human and understandable that people at all levels of an organisation will make different decisions if their job security is threatened.

This may be done consciously or sub-consciously and to different degrees of significance in terms of the overall risks being taken with a project but one thing is for sure, when decisions are made on this basis then additional project risk is an inherent factor.

Let us look at a simple example. A construction company (the contractor) is under pressure from its bankers and the word is around that *'if we don't win these next two or three projects then it is possible the company will go under'*.

So the Bid process for these projects commences and there is immediate pressure from above to subcontractors and suppliers to cut their prices to the bone. Several of these may be owed substantial amounts of money by the contractor and payments have gone out beyond 120 days, which means that the contractor is relying on new projects to sustain cash flow, sometimes referred to by bankers as *'overtrading'*.

The wise thing for the suppliers and subcontractors would be to crystallise their situation right now, possibly accept losses, and not participate, but this depends on how much real information they have on the contractor's financial state; on how large and significant to their business is the money that they are owed; and on the relationships and loyalties they have with the contractor.

So they go ahead and give very competitive quotes. These reach the estimators and planners and mid-level managers. They are all worried about their job security and home mortgages. Even with the best professional and objective assessment it is likely that consciously or sub-consciously they will now make decisions that they otherwise would not have made if the contractor was in a sound financial position.

The Bid proposals reach senior management and the executive directors. Most likely they have a Bid Review Committee. Their situation is probably no different to those lower down the pecking order; maybe it is even worse because of their share holdings and higher salaries and their age insofar as getting another job at a similar level of remuneration will be difficult, especially if they are tainted with the collapse of their previous company.

So the Bid Review Committee takes the view that they will reduce the contingency sums, risk allowances and margins and rely on doing the project efficiently and making some extra margin out of the variations and from further 'screwing' of the suppliers and subcontractors during the course of the project. In reality they are compounding the sharp pencil effect that has already taken place lower down the line.

The Finance Director asks how on earth they can have a positive cash flow on this basis when they still have to provide Performance Guarantees and accept the Retention Sum deductions along the way. He is told that things are going to improve for the contractor generally if they keep winning Bids and the directors will worry about the cash flow situation down the track, after all look at the good 'front-end loading' they are building into the milestone progress payment schedule!

So the contractor wins two new projects on this basis and they commence work. Often, this is when Murphy's Law comes into play and the rest is history.
(See also Chapter 10 – items 8 and 9)

Findings and Recommendations

Summary of Findings - the Bigger Picture

Clients, contractors, consultants and lawyers will all view situations and outcomes from different perspectives – if a major D&C project goes over budget because the contractor has mispriced, then this may not actually be relevant to the client or the consultant (provided he gets paid). They are only interested if they are affected, e.g. the project is late.

Specific risks will therefore be assessed quite differently, depending on who is making the assessment. An objective of this book has been to demonstrate risk management from these different perspectives.

The approach to human dynamics in risk management outlined in this book has been to identify and analyse the human factors and the effects they have in both successful and failed projects and to use this data to revise risk management and control processes in order to substantially reduce the chances of project failure.

Revised processes emanating from this data should enable senior management to better understand and control human behaviour in all phases of the D&C process and result in a far more robust risk management system. This will improve the bidding and delivery processes and greatly reduces the possibility of a construction contract becoming an unexpected financial and reputational disaster.

In summary, the approach outlined:

- Enables senior management to devise more effective risk management processes.
- Provides a bigger-picture understanding to up-and-coming players in the industry at all levels from estimating to site and corporate management.
- Is a valuable aid to recruitment by showing why well-rounded employees require more skills than just technical expertise on the basis that the human aspects are equally or more important than technical skills; it then follows that personal or soft skills should carry significant weight when recruiting and positioning people, whether it be for long term employment or short term for a specific project.
  A strong focus on personnel assessment and positioning has proven to be very beneficial in many organisations in respect of performance, team involvement and job satisfaction.

Findings

- Traditional risk management has failed to provide a practical answer which stops massive project failures.

- Companies expand beyond their capability to control risk management. They spread globally and enter into joint ventures where they lose effective control of the business.

- A new approach is needed which is practical in its application and is applied at the right time, with high level authority.

- A strong focus is needed on compiling a good team of people that take personal responsibility and putting them to work in an environment in which systems and processes support them but do not obviate the need for thought, innovation and hands-on involvement.

- No matter what stage a project has reached, the application of a good practical review or audit of the project is bound to be beneficial and should help to avert a disaster by picking up potential risk issues and preventing them from happening or by mitigating them before much damage is done.

- In the case of project sponsors or investors it is recommended that risk reviews commence at the feasibility stage. In the case of contractors it is recommended that risk review is embedded from the earliest bid stages. In all cases it is recommended that risk reviews are carried out simultaneously by both in-house management and an independent party, with high level sponsorship and reporting lines. Financially, this is not an over-kill. In fact the costs are quite insignificant compared to the cost of a major project and the likely cost overruns if the project turns sour.

- However it is important that budget allowances are made for this from the outset, because if they are not, then inevitably project managers will say they can't afford it.

12 Deadly Sins of Risk Management

The best risk management methodology is absolute efficiency in all areas of a company's operations, in which case the actual risk management check-points should rarely be needed to alert managers to potential risks; however this is not reality and that is why we are writing this book!

At the other end of the 'management efficiency' scale are a number of practices that are just asking for trouble. It is hard enough to run an efficient business operation without being exposed to these types of practices and Boards and CEO's should make it quite clear that they are unacceptable.

1. Inadequate initial planning of the project

   Clients rushing into projects badly prepared; without a clear idea of the concept or the business model; without having conducted proper feasibility studies and having no real idea of the capital costs, operating revenues and costs; no proper procedures or controls in place; with insufficient finance in place because they have nothing tangible to base it on; and then calling tenders and awarding contracts on all this insufficient information, which they justify as taking a 'fast track' approach.

   Do you think this is dreamland and that no one could be that irresponsible? Not at all, as we have shown there have been many examples of this with major projects.

2. Unrealistic programs and budgets

   There are four fairly obvious causes:
   - Inexperience
   - Incompetence
   - People kidding themselves – can only see blue sky
   - Done on purpose for the wrong reasons, e.g. fool the bank or the client; desperate to win the job, etc.

3. Square pegs in round holes

   Project appointments – it is often short-sighted and false economy to employ someone at a rate that meets a budget, with that person falling short of the necessary level of competence, rather than employ someone who can comfortably do the job at the going market rate. The budget needs to be realistic in the first place.

Example: the contract for the design and construction is worth $100m, so any Variations, Liquidated Damages, additional Preliminary costs for program over-runs, etc., are likely to be significant sums, yet some out-of-touch director in the head office has absolutely refused to increase the budget by another $20,000 in order to afford a competent person to run this project; very short-sighted and unrealistic.

There is an excellent truism that says it is cheaper in the long run to employ two really capable people at higher rates than five much cheaper people who do not have the skills and experience.

Cronyism – how often do you see it and how rarely does it work – 'he is a good guy and I can trust him; he is really bright so he will learn how to handle it quickly'; which actually means 'he is a close friend in need of a job and he will do what I tell him without asking awkward questions or rocking the boat'.

4. Lack of cultural understanding and awareness, combined with blatant rudeness

We live in an international world with multi-ethnic populations in most countries and it is completely unacceptable to have managers or any personnel who are not respectful of other nationalities and cultures. If you have a problem in this respect then step aside and let someone else handle it, because your behaviour is likely to be hugely damaging.

5. Arrogance, bullying and out-of-control egos

You will find it from senior managers through to site managers; unfortunately the construction industry has more than its fair share of these people, but there is absolutely no room for it. The great majority of directors and senior managers are not like this and they should not tolerate the culprits.

The problem is that the arrogant bullies become blinded by their own egos and lose insight into the bigger picture. They are generally bad communicators; do not have the respect of their colleagues; and do real damage to relationships.

This sort of person should not be confused with strong, forceful leaders. Often the strong, forceful leaders are also good listeners and communicators and their real strength is in seeing the bigger picture and in implementation.

If you are the boss, before you crack the whip you need to be sitting comfortably in your own saddle, otherwise you might come badly unstuck

6. Buying Projects and Chasing Revenue

On Bid pricing – when times are tough and contracts are hard to get, contractors sometimes bid on a break-even basis in order to recover some corporate overhead costs and keep their teams in work, with a view to making some margin out of variations. This only works if the estimated costs in the Bid are really accurate and the normal contingencies and risk allowances are still kept in the calculations, because under these circumstances you can be sure that Murphy's Law will come into play. Contractors that use this practice are often in financial survival mode anyway.

Chasing revenue – the construction industry is notorious for this, with project managers and design consultants who like to leave *'monuments'* as their legacy. It is often forgotten that on an (average) net margin of say 3% of contract value, if you lose $100m then you have to generate new profitable turnover of $3.3 billion just to make up that loss.

7. <u>Not having an in-depth knowledge of the Contract</u> and understanding the rights and obligations – this is a fundamental sin. It is essential that all key personnel involved in running a project should have a full understanding of the contract.

8. <u>Ignoring Health, Safety and Environmental regulations and standards</u>

    Anyone who has ever been involved with a fatal accident on a construction site will never forget the trauma suffered by the family of the person who died; the sense of loss and de-spiriting effect on the fellow workmates; and the stress of going through lengthy coroners enquiries and in many cases court actions as well.

    It is not difficult to establish the necessary routines and comply strictly with the minimum standards that are in each country. In fact many multi-national companies have minimum standards of their own that are superior to a particular national standard.

    Ignore HS&E or administer it sloppily at your peril. It can ultimately put you out of business. Ensure that your procedures allow for regular independent checking on compliance.

9. <u>Really poor communications</u> – there is no need to elaborate because communications are mentioned repeatedly throughout the book, other than to say that nearly every human and technical problem that arises in a project can be traced back to a breakdown in communications in some form or other somewhere along the line, either verbally or documentary.

10. <u>Bad relationship management</u> – it would seem obvious that all stakeholders participating in a project would want to see a good outcome for all involved and virtually all projects start on that basis, but far too often people start retreating to their corners and putting on their boxing gloves. Good relationship management and communications go hand in hand.

11. <u>Lack of proper control and reporting processes</u> – generally caused by compromise and procrastination in implementing these processes and then a lack of discipline in administering them.

12. **And the Biggest Sin of All – little or no effective risk management!**

    All of the above *'deadly sins'* are risk management items that are related in some way or other to the input of people and responsible management should be constantly on the lookout to ensure they are not occurring.

    Effective risk management will identify these practices at an early stage.

> When you see people acting in a totally irresponsible and outlandish manner and proposing things that seem too good to be true, then they most probably are – and this should form an important part of your risk management assessment.

Conclusion

Personal experiences have been set out in the preceding pages by 13 different people who have been closely involved in construction risk management throughout their careers. Each contributor was requested to write a chapter on a topic of their choice. When you read all these wide-ranging experiences and the views expressed by the authors, it is really noticeable how closely they tie in and coincide with each other on the major points. Whether the descriptions are about successful projects or failed projects, the common thread is always about communication, personnel issues, relationship management and issues relating to human dynamics generally.

These same issues arise on all projects, large and small, and the success or failure of the project very often depends on how these human issues are managed. There are nearly always analyses and post-mortems conducted at the conclusion of a major project, but in many cases they step around the question of the human involvement because it is a case of people reporting on themselves, unless it is done by someone independent, internally or externally.

It is therefore very important to make sure the 'lessons learnt' from projects are passed on to the next project and the next generation, from both successful projects and disastrous ones. One of the main objectives of this book has been to present these experiences in an easy-to-read, concise and practical form for all participants in the industry and in particular we hope that young professionals can take them on board and not learn them the hard way. Managing for success is the over-riding goal.

Construction risk management is really all about people. You need to have the best corporate processes available, but at the end of the day the success or failure of the project will depend on all stakeholders having the right people in the right positions efficiently using the right processes.

Charles O'Neil DipArb FCIArb,
- Director Contract Dynamics Consulting
- Chartered Arbitrator, Mediator, Expert Determiner
- Former Director of Asset Management, Bilfinger Berger Projects S.à r.l Luxembourg

Peter Hansford BSc MBA HonLLD FREng FICE FAPM
- Chief Construction Adviser to the UK Government
- Chairman of the Infrastructure Steering Committee 2010-12
- Visiting Professor, The Bartlett School of Construction & Project Management
- Chairman Engineers Without Borders UK
- President of the Institution of Civil Engineers 2010-2011

Dr Robert Gaitskell QC BSc (Eng.) FIET FIMechE FCIArb
- Keating Chambers, London, UK
- Barrister, Chartered Engineer, Arbitrator, Mediator, Adjudicator, Expert Determiner

Rob Horne LLB, LLM (Dispute Resolution), FCIArb, FSALS
- International Construction Lawyer
- Chartered Arbitrator and Adjudicator
- Tutor and Examiner in Arbitration and Adjudication Law and Practice for RICS and CIArb

John McArthur Dip. Env Pl, BLA
- President, Kiewit Development Company, Omaha, Nebraska, USA

John Messenger MSc BSc CEng FICE FIStructE MAPM
- Director Driver Trett Group

Edward Moore BSc (Hons)
- Chief Executive, ResoLex (Holdings) Limited, UK

David Somerset BSc LLB(Hons) FRICS, FCIArb MEWI
- Managing Director Somerset Consult UK
- Chartered Quantity Surveyor
- Quantum Expert
- Arbitrator, Expert Determiner, Accredited Mediator

Graham Thomson Dip.Elec.Eng, LLB (Hons.)
- CEO, Affinitext Inc.

Stephen Warburton BA(Hons), DipArch, MSc, RIBA
- Former Senior Design Manager, Lend Lease Corporation, UK
- Senior Design Manager, Morgan Sindall plc, Manchester, UK

Dr Anne Watson (BA (Hons), MA, PhD)
- Former curator of architecture and design at the Powerhouse Museum, Sydney
- Author of "Building a Masterpiece: the Sydney Opera House" (2006/2013)

Graham Whitson B.E (Civil) CBA MAppFin
- Managing Director, Bilfinger RE Asset Management (Australia)

Ian Williams MSc DIC CEng FICE FCIArb
- Former Head of Projects for the Government Olympic Executive, London 2012
- Executive Manager for the Supreme Committee for the Qatar 2022 World Cup

APPENDIX B — List of Photos and Diagrams

Chapter

Chapter		
2	1 Photo	Scottish Parliament Building
4	1 Photo	Centennial Bridge, Panama Canal
6	1 Photo	MediacityUK (BBC North)
7	1 Photo	Royal Women's Hospital, Melbourne
8	1 Photo	London Olympic Park
9	2 Photos	Sydney Opera House
12	1 Photo	Tunnel shot
14	1 Chart	Project Crisis – Internal Rapid Escalation Plan
19	2 Photos	Golden Ears Bridge, Vancouver
20	1 Chart	Bid Risk Management Team Structure
21	1 Chart	Typical S-Curve
21	1 Photo	Hamburg Philharmonic Hall

APPENDIX C — Other Academic Papers Relevant to the Theme of this Book

'Delusion & Deception in Large Infrastructure Projects' by Bent Flyvbjerg, Massimo Garbuio, and Dan Lovallo
http://arxiv.org/ftp/arxiv/papers/1303/1303.7403.pdf

'Cost Overruns and Demand Shortfalls in Urban Rail and Other Infrastructure' by Bent Flyvbjerg
http://arxiv.org/ftp/arxiv/papers/1303/1303.7402.pdf

'An Overview of Collaborative Contracting' by Jim Ross, Jim Dingwall and Dr Holly Dinh
http://www.pcigroup.com.au/publications_pci/